Workshop on Companionable Dialogue Systems 2010

(CDS 2010)

Held at ACL 2010

Uppsala, Sweden
15 July 2010

ISBN: 978-1-61738-811-8

Printed from e-media with permission by:

Curran Associates, Inc.
57 Morehouse Lane
Red Hook, NY 12571

Some format issues inherent in the e-media version may also appear in this print version.

Printed by Curran Associates, Inc. (2010)

Association for Computational Linguistics
209 N. Eighth Street
Stroudsburg, Pennsylvania 18360

Phone: 1-570-476-8006
Fax: 1-570-476-0860

acl@aclweb.org

Additional copies of this publication are available from:

Curran Associates, Inc.
57 Morehouse Lane
Red Hook, NY 12571 USA
Phone: 845-758-0400
Fax: 845-758-2634
Email: curran@proceedings.com
Web: www.proceedings.com

Introduction

The current state of dialogue technology has come a long way since its beginning in the 1950s: dialogue technology now provides interactive service agents, while research explores various aspects of multimodal and multiparty communication so as to improve natural and social aspects of dialogue systems. In this workshop, interest is focussed especially on dialogue systems able to act as Companions, i.e. software agents with advanced human language technology capacities, able to display and recognise emotion and aspects of personality as well as to interact with a user, possibly over a long period, learning about their needs and interests, performing services, entertaining, consoling, and so on. The focus of the workshop is on text and speech aspects of dialogue with Companions, but topics to be discussed also include the impact of non-dialogue phenomena (e.g., presence, low-level control and recognition, avatar technology, etc.) on dialogue and the interaction of other modalities with dialogue.

Dialogue technology has two main historical sources, both still of relevance today: first, the chatbot tradition going back at least to ELIZA and PARRY and, secondly, the task-driven knowledge-based system back to at least BASEBALL and SHRDLU, all these examples being from the late 1960s. The great chatbots of the past, which bear little relationship to the current rash of Internet products, did have some claim to companionableness of a sort, and e.g. PARRY had explicit emotion parameters of fear and anger that affected its outputs. The chatbots sometimes left initiative with the user (like ELIZA which initiated nothing) and sometimes with the system (like PARRY, who had long paranoid stories to tell if given a chance). The task-based systems, however, aimed at efficient task completion with little attention paid to the social or emotional aspects of interaction. The initiative was always with the user and the system was regarded as a tool or servant with no goal other than to answer or carry out a task as efficiently it could.

The two kind of systems gave rise to quite different forms of evaluation as well: the chatbots led to the sophisticated but artificial "Turing Test" environment of the Loebner competition, while the funded and deployed task-systems — of which the best known were the MIT airline reservation systems like PEGASUS and JUPITER — were evaluated in competitions in terms of time and completion of task rates. However, comparison between systems and their performance proved difficult; no generally applicable and agreed evaluation framework or methodology is available for the companionable systems we are interested in this workshop. A central question then is whether it is possible to measure companionship, and if so, whether is it possible to include some aspects of it in the evaluation of dialogue systems?

Although both the chatbot and task-based traditions began as text-only systems, they were able to take advantage of the rapid advances in speech technology, and fuse speech and language research increasingly. However, none of this led to any obvious advance in what is the goal of this workshop: the exploration of research advances in dialogue systems able to act as Companions. It seems clear that both early traditions have much to contribute to the goal of a Companion, and that it cannot be founded exclusively on either alone. Thus the paper by **Shaikh et al.** takes the analysis of social behaviour in human Internet chat dialogue data as the starting point for building a more sophisticated virtual chat agent.

Many advances have been expected and achieved in pursuing the overall goal of a Companions in recent years, including the increasing sophistication of ASR and language generation and their integration with NLP and with higher-level issues of emotion and dialogue control. However, that there still is room for further improvements in these areas is exemplified in the contribution by **Wallis**.

Other advances vital to the notion of Companionship have come from more sophisticated dialogue management models based on representations of the agents' previous experiences — such as the work presented by **Sieber & Krenn** on episodic memory — and/or personalisation based on the representation of the knowledge about the user, as in the paper by **Adam, Cavedon & Padgham**.

Further advances have been made in a range of deployable theories of emotion that can be connected directly to text and speech, as well as to facial expressions of talking heads as discussed by **Powers et al**. The work by **Konstantopoulos** also discusses the use of emotions, on both the user and the agent side, in the context of furthering the feeling of personalisation, while **Pulman et al.** let the analysis of the emotions of the user guide the dialogue management process of the agent.

Also, many recent improvement in Companion-like system come from the use of new techniques of content extraction in dialogue (such as Information Extraction) and, like every other part of language technology, from the steady advance of machine learning techniques and associated evaluation methods, as shown in several of the presentations in the workshop.

One of the aims of the workshop is to be a forum for focussed discussion of what it is to give a convincing and useful illusion of "personality" in a long-term Companion, when that is advantageous and when not. The paper by **Wilks** discusses some of these concepts using the role of the Victorian lady's Companion as a key metaphor.

The primary aim of the workshop is to explore and discuss promising new methods to design and evaluate dialogue systems able to act as Companions, as well as to report and review recent advances in a wide range of Companion-related topics, concentrating on the what the precise role of language and speech technology is in achieving this. To this end, the first presentation of the workshop is an invited talk by **Traum** on the "Do's and Don'ts for Software Companions".

Welcome to the ACL 2010 Workshop on Companionable Dialogue Systems!

Yorick Wilks
Florida Institute of Human and Machine Cognition,
Pensacola, Florida, US

Björn Gambäck
SICS, Swedish Institute of Computer Science AB, Kista, SE
Norwegian University of Science and Technology, Trondheim, NO

Morena Danieli
Loquendo Voice Technologies —
Telecom Italia, Torino, IT

Organizers:

Yorick Wilks, Florida Institute of Human and Machine Cognition, US
Björn Gambäck, SICS, Swedish Institute of Computer Science AB, SE *and* Norwegian University of Science and Technology, NO
Morena Danieli, Loquendo Voice Technologies — Telecom Italia, Torino, IT

Program Committee:

Jan Alexandersson, DFKI, DE
James Allen, IHMC, US
Elizabeth Andre, University of Augsburg, DE
David Benyon, Napier University, UK
Harry Bunt, University of Tilburg, NL
Morena Danieli, Loquendo, IT
Björn Gambäck, SICS, SE / NTNU, NO
Pavel Ircing, University of West Bohemia, CZ
Kristiina Jokinen, University of Helsinki, FI
Anton Nijholt, University of Twente, NL
Tim Paek, Microsoft, US
Candy Sidner, Worcester Polytechnic Institute, US
Tomek Strzalkowski, Albany University, US
David Traum, USC-ICT, US
Markku Turunen, University of Tampere, FI
Nick Webb, Albany University, US
Yorick Wilks, Florida Institute of Human and Machine Cognition, US
Enrico Zovato, Loquendo, IT
Ingrid Zukerman, Monash University, OZ

Invited Speaker:

David Traum, Institute for Creative Technologies, US

Table of Contents

Conference Program

Thursday, July 15, 2010

09:00–10:30 Invited Paper Session

09:00–09:15 Welcome

09:15–10:30 Invited Paper

Do's and Don'ts for Software Companions, by David Traum

10:30–11:00 Morning Break

Session I (11:00–12:30)

11:00–11:30 *Episodic Memory for Companion Dialogue*
Gregor Sieber and Brigitte Krenn

11:30–12:00 *MANA for the Ageing*
David M W Powers, Martin H Luerssen, Trent W Lewis, Richard E Leibbrandt, Marissa Milne, John Pashalis and Kenneth Treharne

12:00–12:30 *Is a Companion a Distinctive Kind of Relationship with a Machine?*
Yorick Wilks

12:30–14:00 Lunch Break

Session II (14:00–15:30)

14:00–14:30 *"Hello Emily, How Are You Today?" - Personalised Dialogue in a Toy to Engage Children.*
Carole Adam, Lawrence Cavedon and Lin Padgham

14:30–15:00 *A Robot in the Kitchen*
Peter Wallis

15:00–15:30 *An Embodied Dialogue System with Personality and Emotions*
Stasinos Konstantopoulos

Thursday, July 15, 2010 (continued)

15:30–16:00 Afternoon Break

Session III (16:00–17:00)

16:00–16:30 *How Was Your Day?*
Stephen Pulman, Johan Boye, Marc Cavazza, Cameron Smith and Raúl Santos de la Cámara

16:30–17:00 *VCA: An Experiment with a Multiparty Virtual Chat Agent*
Samira Shaikh, Tomek Strzalkowski, Sarah Taylor and Nick Webb

17:00–17:30 Wrap up discussion of the day's issues

Workshop ends (17:30)

Episodic Memory for Companion Dialogue

Gregor Sieber
OFAI
Vienna, Austria
gregor.sieber@ofai.at

Brigitte Krenn
OFAI
Vienna, Austria
brigitte.krenn@ofai.at

Abstract

We present an episodic memory component for enhancing the dialogue of artificial companions with the capability to refer to, take up and comment on past interactions with the user, and to take into account in the dialogue long-term user preferences and interests. The proposed episodic memory is based on RDF representations of the agent's experiences and is linked to the agent's semantic memory containing the agent's knowledge base of ontological data and information about the user's interests.

1 Introduction

Recently, research on artificial companions has come more and more in focus. They are artificial agents (virtual or robotic) that are intended to support the human user in aspects of everyday life. They may range from virtual agents that assist their users in accessing information from the Internet in accordance with the users' interests, preferences and needs (Skowron et al., 2008), up to assistive robots in home environments that support elderly in mastering their life at home (Graf et al., 2009). In the long run when developing companions, the goal is to model and implement artificial "caring developing helpers" (Sloman, 2007) that learn and develop over time to be of long-term benefit for the user.

In order to come closer to the vision of artificial companions a number of research issues need to be addressed such as: action-perception and learning capabilities suitable to function with imperfect sensors in dynamically changing environments which can only be partially modelled; the development of affect sensing capabilities that extend over the detection of basic emotions such as joy, anger, fear, disgust etc. (Ekman, 1992); user models that account for and adapt to the users' interests, preferences, affective states, needs and handicaps; approaches to multimodal dialogue that allow the agent's mental models and memories to be connected to its expressive behaviour (Castellano et al., 2008), and where natural language dialogue is semantically grounded (Benyon and Mival, 2008). Companions need to be aware of their own history and past interactions with their individual users, so that the single user can believe that her/his companion knows "what it is talking about". This is particularly important for creating acceptable long–term interactions.

To account for this kind of requirements, we propose a communication component for companions where autobiographic episodic memory, semantic memory and dialogue are closely connected. In our approach, input analysis is performed using information extraction techniques, that yield RDF triples describing the content of a user utterance in terms of the knowledge base (semantic memory) of the companion, and an utterance class describing the type of message (greeting, question, agreement, rejection, etc.). Short term memory holds the current user utterance and a set of pointers to currently important and thus activated parts of the companion's knowledge. We distinguish two parts of the long term memory: *Semantic memory* is composed of a knowledge base containing ontological data and a user model encoding e.g. elements of the ontology which the user is especially interested in. *Episodic memory* is based on RDF representations of the agent's experiences. It contains utterances of the user and the companion, and representations of the companion's actions and their evaluation (for the cases where it is known). The dialogue manager consists of a set of parallel, independent components for the different queries on the episodic memory described below and answer retrieval from the knowledge base. Which component is finally used

Proceedings of the 2010 Workshop on Companionable Dialogue Systems, ACL 2010, pages 1–6,
Uppsala, Sweden, 15 July 2010.

is decided by a scoring mechanism in connection with a rule set.

In the remainder of this contribution, we will concentrate on the interplay between episodic memory and dialogue. In particular, we describe how the episodic memory is represented (sec. 2), how episodes are retrieved (sec. 3), and how natural language output is generated from memory content (sec. 4).

2 Episodic Memory Representation

An episodic memory component for companion dialogue needs to provide adequate knowledge representation in connection with the cognitive model and the tasks of the agent. RDF-based[1] data stores are widely used for representing domain knowledge as well as common sense knowledge (e.g. the Open Mind Common Sense Database[2], or ConceptNet[3]). Accordingly, we have developed an episodic memory component for artificial companions that stores episodes as RDF graphs. Since both memory, domain and common sense knowledge bases are composed of RDF triples, they are interoperable and can be easily extended. We use a Sesame[4] repository for hosting the data stores.

Episode encoding is automatic, since all user input and its analysis is immediately transferred from short-term memory to episodic memory. Thus the agent is able to recall the same data from an episode that was available at the time of the experience.

For episode retrieval, a similarity matching algorithm is required that can find memories based on similarity of the individuals and relations involved. Thus, our retrieval mechanism neither treats the RDF data as symbols in a similarity vector – such as for a nearest–neighbour search –, nor as a graph matching problem, which often is too slow for retrieval. Both of these approaches do not take advantage of the RDF encoding of the data, and as a consequence do not allow class or superclass information of individuals to be used for matching.

Our approach is to query the RDF repositories using a query language such as SeRQL and SPARQL. While these query languages do not allow a direct search for a similar graph, a set of queries can be generated from a target episode making use of the full range of features of RDF and the query language. The episode most similar to the input episode is then selected from the result set by applying a heuristic.

2.1 Episodes

In our system, there are several types of episodes which share a set of basic parameters, each representing the different events and actions in the world of the agent.

The different sub-types of episodes are RDF subclasses of the basic episode concept and contain specialised parameters applicable to the type of action.

Basic properties stored with each episode are: a) *creation time* of the episode and b) an *episode ID* property which is used to trace back or forward through the episodes in (reverse) order of creation, to find the outcome and evaluation following an episode retrieved from memory. This is necessary, because triples in RDF are stored as graphs and not database entries like in a relational database which could easily be ordered by a primary key.

Action episodes are a subclass of episodes that represent the actions the agent is capable of. These are:
Answer from domain knowledge the agent maps the user's question to a SeRQL query and evaluates the query against its domain knowledge base.
Find similar interactions represents deliberate remembering, i.e. actively searching for similar situations.
Pattern search allows the agent to check for a set of patterns in the behaviour of the user and its episodic memory which can be exploited for dialogue.
Retrieve context is employed by the agent when no other actions can be applied because parts of the utterance are missing. The companion then searches its memories to retrieve relevant context of the dialogue.
Send message to the user, which can either communicate the results of a query, memories of the agent, statements based on results from pattern search, or details about the situation of the agent, which includes reporting errors.

Input episodes store textual user input. They contain the analysis of the user input which is an RDF description of the entities, classes and prop-

[1] http://www.w3.org/RDF/
[2] http://commons.media.mit.edu/en/
[3] http://conceptnet.media.mit.edu/
[4] http://www.openrdf.org/

erties of the domain ontology contained in the utterance. For example, the question "When was Charlie Parker born?" is classified as utterance class WH-Question, and its analysis is an RDF triple with the ontology individual of class *Artist* representing Charlie Parker, the property *birthDate*, and a variable as the object since it is this value the user wants to know.

Evaluation episodes can be either positive or negative. They are crucial for the agent to be able to learn from its past actions. If an evaluation is available, the agent can decide based on its memories whether a past solution should be repeated or not. Not all episodes have an evaluation. Evaluation values can either come from direct user feedback or internal feedback such as empty query results or failure to retrieve a query result.

In order to be able to find the right associations and memories, the agent also needs to have an internal notion of *relative time* that can be related to interactions with the user. As noted e.g. by Brom and Lukavský (2009) humans commonly do not use exact times, but instead refer to fuzzy categories. Thus, our (application specific) time model of the companion allows to differentiate between four coarse times of day – morning, noon, afternoon, evening. For events that are further in the past, the model contains the categories of: today, yesterday, this week, this month, this year, last year.

2.2 Episode Dynamics

Due to available computing hardware and scalable triple stores, the episodic memory component is technically able to store a large amount of memories. But when the episode base grows too big, it becomes increasingly difficult to retrieve episodes within an acceptable time limit due to the growing number of search and comparison operations required. Thus the companion needs a mechanism of reducing the number of episodes in the memory. Generally, there are two approaches to this: episode blending and forgetting.

Episode blending refers to a mechanism that groups similar experiences into one episode. Less important parameters of the memories are lost, and the similarities strengthened. This would mean the agent can remember what happened, and that it happened more than once, but the exact situations are lost. Episode blending is an interesting aspect of episodic memory that will be pursued in our future work.

Forgetting refers to the deletion of episodes. Ideally, the episodes with least utility to the companion should be deleted. Nuxoll (2007) provides a list of possible approaches regarding forgetting: 1) remove the oldest memory first, 2) remove the least activated memory, 3) remove the most redundant memory, 4) memory decay.

Approach 1) does not take the importance of episodes into account and may result in losing important information. Approaches 2) and 4) both depend on assigning activation values to episodes, and delete those with the least activation. The idea of 3) is to locate two memories that are very similar to each other and remove one of them.

Our initial strategy is to assign a time-stamp of last retrieval to each episode, since we currently do not use activation values. Episode removal can then be regularly performed by issuing a SeRQL delete statement for all episodes whose retrieval date is older than a certain time, depending on the growth rate of the memory.

Note that the removal process described above still bears the risk of losing important memories of situations that are very rarely encountered. For our dialogue application scenario, this risk might not seem too critical, yet it might be e.g. for an agent in an artificial life environment where seldomly occurring enemies need to be recognised. A possible remedy would be the connection of episodic memory with a model of emotion. This would allow the emotional intensity of a situation to be a factor in episode retrieval and deletion.

3 Retrieval of Episodic Memories

One of the important aspects of any episodic memory component is to retrieve the right memories.

Since our episodic memory is realised using RDF, a set of SeRQL queries is used for episode retrieval. Queries are processed in parallel. The construction of these queries depends on the type of episode represented by the input situation.

The following section describes our model for deliberate retrieval for dialogue situations. This means that the companion actively chooses to search its memory for episodes of relevance.

The current situation is characterised by a set of features, expressed in RDF data, that are extracted from short term memory: 1) the description of the user utterance in terms of domain data, 2) the current time, 3) a list of entities in the user utterance that are among the user's preferred entities, if any.

A query is issued representing the input situation. This means, we search the memory to see if the exact same situation has been encountered previously. Alternatively, queries using combinations and subsets of the instance set and the set of relations present in the user utterance are issued. For instance, given a popular music gossipping scenario, if the user asks a question about Michael Jackson, Janet Jackson, and Tina Turner, the agent searches its memory for previous episodes involving the named artists and relations or subsets of those, in order to connect to and take up previous discussions. Moreover, the structure of the domain data is used for generating a query containing the classes of the individuals in the utterance. For example, an agent that has talked about the birthday of any guitar player before, could relate a user question about the birthday of Joe Satriani to the previous experience by knowing that he is a guitar player too, and use this knowledge in the ongoing dialogue.

Queries related to classes can be iterated by following up the superclass hierarchy until a result is found. The iteration stops either when there is no further superclass, or when the property under discussion is not a property of the superclass any more. For example, talking about the birthday of an *Artist*, the companion looks for episodes about birthdays involving its superclass *Person*, but not episodes with its superclass *Entity*, since the class *Entity* has no birthday property.

The most similar episode is selected from the result set by a heuristic which ranks those episodes higher that resemble the input episode more closely, so for example an episode that contains the same entities and the same properties as the input episode is ranked higher than an episode that contains a matching entity with a different property, and so on.

These content–driven retrieval strategies can be used to support the selection of the next dialogue move, taking into account available evaluations of similar past episodes. Additionally to the content–driven mechanism of remembering, the companion can also search its memories for recency- and preference-driven patterns that can be used for dialogue, such as the following examples. In contrast to the mechanisms mentioned above, these operations are automatically performed without requiring the agent's initiative.

Has the same question been discussed recently, or ever before? The companion can make a comment to the user about this – either noting as trivia that the question has been asked a year ago, or reacting annoyed if the user asks the same question for the fifth time within ten minutes.

Is there a property in a user utterance that is among the user's interests? Has this property been asked for in the last 15 interactions? For example, the user is very interested in the birth places of artists. The companion can use this information in the following ways: a) for the next artist under discussion, automatically provide the birth place to the user; b) the companion can comment on the fact that the property is part of the user interests; c) the companion can ask the user whether she would like to know the birthplace of a randomly selected artist from her preference list (the companion would select an artist whose birth place has not been inquired in the recent past, by checking against its memories).

In the last 15 interactions that related to a certain property, is there a strong tendency (currently, more than 66%) towards one specific value of that property? The companion can then search for similar cases among the data, and check whether there is another artist – maybe even among the user's preferred artists – that shares this birth place.

Additionally, this type of information is stored in the user model and leads to automatic retrieval of episodes where appropriate. Continuing the example of the birth place from above: a day after being asked about artists born in New York, the companion might notice while talking about the albums recorded by Billy Joel that he was also born in New York, and communicate it to the user.

Building upon the user preferences stored in the user model, the remembering process additionally contains queries related to the most prevalent preferences of the user model. This is similar to finding strengthened links in a connectionist model. For example, if one of the currently high-ranked user preferences is *asking for information about artists born in New York*, a query is automatically generated from the user model to look for this information connected to the individuals in the input graph.

4 Output Generation

Since our companion "thinks" in RDF statements, it requires mechanisms to communicate their content to the user. We distinguish two classes of RDF statements from which to generate natural-language output. The first class is RDF data that describes content from the domain ontologies, e.g, that Duke Ellington was born in Washington, DC. The second class are statements that describe a certain type of communicative intent, such as telling the user that she just asked the same question as five minutes ago.

Our approach for the second case is that of template–based generation, where each communicative intent from the ontology corresponds to a different template. The templates are described using the Velocity[5] template language, and can thus be extended separately from the program code, while still offering the possibility to make use of memory contents for filling slots in the templates.

The first case is handled by directly generating a sentence structure from the subject – predicate – object structure of the RDF graph. Triples are sorted by subject; subjects that also appear as objects are inserted as relative clauses. Statements that share the same subject are connected by coordination or relative clauses, depending on the type of relation, and so forth. The input may contain negation markers, which are realised as negative polarity items.

The surface string of predicates is generated by using a set of templates and morphological processing (e.g. pluralisation). For subjects and objects, a query on the knowledge base is performed to retrieve an adequate natural language representation. For example, while the name of a person is in the *name* property of the *Person* class, the name of a music album is contained in the property *albumTitle*. A mapping for each class to such a property is stored in an annotation file.

5 Related Work

Catizone et al. (2008) use an extended version of GATE's ANNIE subsystem, combined with a set of gazetteers, to identify relationships in the input to their Senior Companion system. The focus of the Senior Companion is to use the data extracted from the user utterances to collect information about the user's life. While our input analysis system is similar, it uses regular expression patterns over annotations for the matching of relations between, and properties of, individuals and classes. In terms of functionality, our system focuses on being able to answer user requests and provide continued dialogue by taking into account the previous interactions with the user.

Episodic memory has first been distinguished from other memory types by Tulving (1972). Implementations have for example been used in artificial life agents (Nuxoll, 2007; Ho et al., 2003), in storytelling agents (Ho et al., 2007; Ho and Dautenhahn, 2008), and for non-player characters in games (Brom et al., 2007; Brom and Lukavský, 2009). Since our memory component is realised as an RDF graph, nearest–neighbour search as in the memory model proposed by Nuxoll (2007) does not directly apply.

Brom and Lukavský (2009) summarise important aspects of episodic memory and propose a more detailed concept of time categories than ours. In contrast to their work, our memory is not concerned with remembering locations, but with finding items relevant for current dialogue in the episodic memory of the agent, and thus stores different data.

Both the adaptive mind agent by Krenn et al. (2009) and Gossip Galore (Xu et al., 2009) describe companion systems able to answer questions on domain data. Both agents only have limited knowledge of their own past and do not use it for dialogue. Thus they cannot ground dialogue in their own experiences, and are unable to leverage knowledge about user preferences for providing more interesting dialogue.

Cavazza et al. (2008) describe a companion system for helping users plan a healthier lifestyle. Dialogue can be driven by the companion or by the user, but revolves around agreeing upon a daily exercise plan or negotiating re-planning in case of plan failure. Our system aims at a more open kind of dialogue which does not revolve around a plan model. Instead, the user is able to ask different kinds of questions on all the domain data available, which leaves the companion in a situation where much less expectations can be made towards the next user utterance.

6 Conclusion

We have presented a model of a companion that uses an RDF–based episodic memory component for enhancing dialogue with the user and grounding domain knowledge in interaction experiences interconnected with the agent's knowledge base.

[5] http://velocity.apache.org/

The full implementation of the model is currently work in progress.

Retrieval of episodes is accomplished by using a set of competing SeRQL queries. Our model shows how the contents of past interactions and their relation to current dialogue can be employed by a companion for selecting the next dialogue move and generating dialogue content.

Acknowledgements

The work presented is supported by the Austrian Ministry for Transport, Innovation and Technology (BMVIT) under the programme "FEMtech Women in Research and Technology" grant nr. 821855, project C4U. The Austrian Research Institute for Artificial Intelligence (OFAI) is supported by the Austrian ministries BMVIT and BMWF.

References

David Benyon and Oli Mival. 2008. Scenarios for companions. In *Austrian Artificial Intelligence Workshop*, September.

Cyril Brom and Jirí Lukavský. 2009. Towards Virtual Characters with a Full Episodic Memory II: The Episodic Memory Strikes Back. In *Proc. Empathic Agents, AAMAS workshop*, pages 1–9.

Cyril Brom, Klára Pesková, and Jirí Lukavský. 2007. Towards characters with a full episodic memory. In Catherine Pelachaud, Jean-Claude Martin, Elisabeth André, Gérard Chollet, Kostas Karpouzis, and Danielle Pelé, editors, *IVA*, volume 4722 of *Lecture Notes in Computer Science*, pages 360–361. Springer.

G. Castellano, R. Aylett, K. Dautenhahn, A. Paiva, P. W. McOwan, and S. Ho. 2008. Long-Term Affect Sensitive and Socially Interactive Companions. In *Proceedings of the 4th International Workshop on Human-Computer Conversation*.

Roberta Catizone, Alexiei Dingli, Hugo Pinto, and Yorick Wilks. 2008. Information extraction tools and methods for understanding dialogue in a companion. In *Proceedings of the Sixth International Language Resources and Evaluation (LREC'08)*.

Marc Cavazza, Cameron Smith, Daniel Charlton, Li Zhang, Markku Turunen, and Jaakko Hakulinen. 2008. A 'companion' ECA with planning and activity modelling. In *AAMAS '08: Proceedings of the 7th international joint conference on Autonomous agents and multiagent systems*, pages 1281–1284.

Paul Ekman. 1992. An argument for basic emotions. *Cognition and Emotion*, 6:169–200.

Birgit Graf, Ulrich Reiser, Martin Hägele, Kathrin Mauz, and Peter Klein. 2009. Robotic home assistant care-o-bot 3 - product vision and innovation platform. In *IEEE / Robotics and Automation Society: IEEE Workshop on Advanced Robotics and its Social Impacts - ARSO 2009*, pages 139–144, New York, NY, USA. Piscataway.

Wan Ching Ho and Kerstin Dautenhahn. 2008. Towards a narrative mind: The creation of coherent life stories for believable virtual agents. In *IVA '08: Proceedings of the 8th international conference on Intelligent Virtual Agents*, pages 59–72, Berlin, Heidelberg. Springer.

Wan Ching Ho, Kerstin Dautenhahn, and Chrystopher L. Nehaniv. 2003. Comparing different control architectures for autobiographic agents in static virtual environments. In Thomas Rist, Ruth Aylett, Daniel Ballin, and Jeff Rickel, editors, *IVA*, volume 2792 of *Lecture Notes in Computer Science*, pages 182–191. Springer.

Wan Ching Ho, João Dias, Rui Figueiredo, and Ana Paiva. 2007. Agents that remember can tell stories: integrating autobiographic memory into emotional agents. In Edmund H. Durfee, Makoto Yokoo, Michael N. Huhns, and Onn Shehory, editors, *AAMAS*, page 10. IFAAMAS.

Brigitte Krenn, Marcin Skowron, Gregor Sieber, Erich Gstrein, and Jörg Irran. 2009. Adaptive mind agent. In *IVA '09: Proceedings of the 9th International Conference on Intelligent Virtual Agents*, pages 519–520, Berlin, Heidelberg. Springer.

Andrew Nuxoll. 2007. *Enhancing Intelligent Agents with Episodic Memory*. Ph.D. thesis, Univ. of Michigan, Ann Arbor.

Marcin Skowron, Jörg Irran, and Brigitte Krenn. 2008. Computational framework for and the realization of cognitive agents providing intelligent assistance capabilities. In *18th European Conference on Artificial Intelligence, Cognitive Robotics Workshop*, pages 88–96.

Aaron Sloman. 2007. Requirements for Digital Companions It's harder than you think. In *Position Paper for Workshop on Artificial Companions in Society: Perspectives on the Present and Future*. Oxford Internet Institute.

Endel Tulving. 1972. Episodic and semantic memory. In E. Tulving and W. Donaldson, editors, *Organization of Memory*, pages 381–403. Academic Press, New York.

Feiyu Xu, Peter Adolphs, Hans Uszkoreit, Xiwen Cheng, and Hong Li. 2009. Gossip galore: A conversational web agent for collecting and sharing pop trivia. In Joaquim Filipe, Ana L. N. Fred, and Bernadette Sharp, editors, *ICAART*, pages 115–122. INSTICC Press.

MANA for the Ageing

David M W Powers, Martin H Luerssen, Trent W Lewis, Richard E Leibbrandt, Marissa Milne, John Pashalis and Kenneth Treharne
AI Lab, School of Computer Science, Engineering and Mathematics,
Flinders University, South Australia
David.Powers@flinders.edu.au

Abstract

We present a family of Embodied Conversational Agents (ECAs) using Talking Head technology, along with a program of associated research and user trials. Whilst antecedents of our current ECAs include "chatbots" desgined to pass the Turing Test (TT) or win a Loebner Prize (LP), our current agents are task-oriented Teaching Agents and Social Companions. The current focus for our research includes the role of emotion, expression and gesture in our agents/companions, the explicit teaching of such social skills as recognizing and displaying appropriate expressions/gestures, and the integration of template/database-based dialogue managers with more conversational TT/LP systems as well as with audio-visual speech/gesture recognition/synthesis technologies.

1 Introduction

Embodied Conversational Agents (ECAs) are animated or robotic agents that engage users in real-time dialogue. As a development of the Chatterbot TT/LP system, they address a fundamental criticism of the Turing Test (TT) as incarnated in the Loebner Prize (LP), viz. the lack of understanding of the world, the lack of understanding people, the lack of personality (Harnad,1992; Shapiro,1992). This has in fact been acknowledge by Loebner who has insisted that more than "pen pal" conversation is necessary to win his $100K prize and Gold medal, and arranged design of a multimodal test [3]. At a technological level ECAs are a showcase for a large variety of language and human interface technologies including speech and face recognition and synthesis, speech understanding and generation, and dialogue management. However, at a deeper level they are a platform for exploring affect – the effect of multimodal features, including in particular expression and gesture on the human user.

Our aim is not to pass the Turing Test, although perhaps some descendant of our system will eventually do so. Rather our focus is to provide an effective agent for specific tasks where the limitations of current conversational companions, or dialog technologies, serve to match rather than conflict with the application constraints. Whereas limiting the topic was seen as a trick and a cheat in the Loebner Prize, our aim is to demonstrate and develop useful technologies and we are not interested in philosophical debates about intelligence. For these naturally constrained applications human level grammatical and syntactic understanding is not required, and the simple ELIZA-like approach of template matching is perfectly adequate as a first step (Weizenbaum, 1966).

Our initial Talking Head was based around the Stelarc Prosthetic Head[1] which combines multiple off-the-shelf components: keyboard input to a chatbot (*AliceBot*[2]) is linked to speech synthesis (*IBM ViaVoice*[3]) and 3D face rendering (*Eyematic*[4]). More recently we have adopted Head X[5] which is capable of generating a continuous, synchronized, optionally subtitled audiovisual speech stream in many different languages, with the ability to switch and modify voices and morph different faces at the same time as interacting with the user. The system is designed to be able to use different speech and face technologies, and we in general use Microsoft's SAPI[6] for speech recognition and generation plus the FaceGen face generation technology[7].

[1] http://www.stelarc.va.com.au/prosthetichead/
[2] http://www.alicebot.org/about.html
[3] http://www.ibm.com/software/pervasive/viavoice.html
[4] http://google.about.com/od/n/g/nevenvisiondef.htm
[5] http://csem.flinders.edu.au/research/programs/th/
[6] http://msdn.microsoft.com/speech
[7] http://www.facegen.com

Proceedings of the 2010 Workshop on Companionable Dialogue Systems, ACL 2010, pages 7–12,
Uppsala, Sweden, 15 July 2010. ©2010 Association for Computational Linguistics

2 Teaching ECA Applications

We have been predominantly exploring the application of our Talking Head as a virtual tutor of various subject areas. Initially our focus was language teaching/learning, but more recently demand for assistance with social teaching and assistant/companion applications has redirected our efforts.

The Talking Head has been extended for teaching and environmental/social interaction purposes with intelligent software that integrates inputs from various input sources such as cameras, microphones, touch sensors, and the like. A situational model is constructed that represents the physical environment in which encounters with the user take place. A teaching application can monitor a student's spoken utterances using both audio and video, can try to identify the student's facial expressions, and can make reference to physical objects in the surroundings (including specially-devised teaching 'props').

In addition to spoken utterances (the principal mode of output used in these applications), the Head may make use of audiovisual content presented on additional computer monitors and provide non-linguistic output that involves other sensory modalities, e.g. by making use of haptic devices. The multimodal capabilities of our ECA Teaching Agent are particularly valuable as they allow tutor and student to ground their interaction in a shared physical and social environment. Another invaluable aspect of our ECA for language teaching is the ability to model a student speaking the target language with a correct accent and authentic facial expression and gestures, with their own face and voice.

It is important in teaching, and in particular in language teaching, not to give the student any examples of incorrect or poor grammar, accent, etc. In a classroom context, students are held back and given poor example by other students, as well as by teachers who are not native speakers. Seeing or hearing their own incorrect written or spoken examples is immensely counterproductive. A good language teacher will reflect back, with appropriate degree of inflectional and gestural approbation, what they have said in corrected form. Having a close-up face as well as a voice to emulate allows unconscious recognition of the cultural and linguistic characteristics that are part of language, including the way of holding the mouth that affects even the way a person pauses or pronounces a neutral vowel sound, as well as the whole vowel system. With languages that have new consonants or vowels, or different variants that are treated as allophonic in their first language, seeing how those sounds are made can be very important to achieving an authentic accent. Body language, hand gesture, volume and tone, are all parts of this that are beyond the competence of current speech recognition and synthesis. This ability for our ECA to control vocal and gestural 'accent' is thus a primary focus of our research.

One specific application of the Language Teaching Agent is for teaching children with a partial or complete hearing impairment to speak and lipread, where the face rather than the voice is their primary cue. A related one is for teaching corresponding speaking and signing skills to their families. A third is for teaching literacy to indigenous children who have reasonable verbal competence in English (in our case) as a national language, as well as their tribal language and often a trade language as a first and second language.

Preliminary trials with comprehension testing found that appropriate facial expressions could enhance performance by a full grade point (Related-reference, 2008). However, it also identified that inappropriate expressions could negate this advantage – in particular it seemed that in one case the ECA was seen as laughing at rather than laughing with the subject matter. This has required us to modify our emotion model to include humour with both positive and negative affect. Moreover the emotional markup was performed by hand by one of the authors. We are currently engaged in a complex sequence of staged trials to develop appropriate ways of eliciting the desired AV expressions, getting multiple people to markup the texts, getting multiple subjects to classify and evaluate both real and head expressions, prior to undertaking a more comprehensive range of evaluations with the newly developed texts and markups, as well as a human head baseline. Currently there is very little in the way of audiovisual (as opposed to single image only) corpora of spontaneous or acted emotions and expressions.

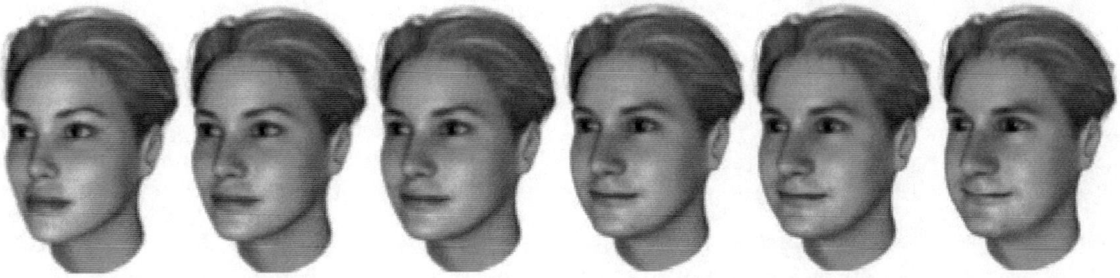

Figure 1. Example of FaceGen morphing: female to male. Morphing is also used to provide speech gestures/visemes, emotion gestures/expressions, as well as explicit gestures like winks.

2.1 Social Tutors for Children

Once we started working with organizations that provided assistance to those with various disabilities and disadvantages, a major common factor emerged: the social problems that go with the disability or with looking different, or even just being from a different social or cultural background. Social skills tutoring of children with autism, hearing impairment and other disorders looks to be a promising application of our ECA Teaching Agent, which can accurately model facial expressions, and whose appearance and interactions can be customized to meet learners' needs. Initially we have focused on children with Autism Spectrum Disorders and our initial trials are in this ASD community.

Individuals with autism typically lack the skills needed to participate successfully in everyday social interactions, particularly reading nonverbal cues. Additionally, sufferers often feel more comfortable learning through technology than with other people, who may be judgmental or unpredictable.

Two lesson sequences reflecting common difficulties for children with autism were developed, the first on basic conversation skills and the second on managing bullying. There was a 54% average improvement from pre- to post-testing for the managing bullying module and a 32% average improvement for the conversation skills module, showing clearly that learning can take place through this method (Related-Reference, 2009).

3 Independent Living for the Ageing

The Memory, Appointment and Navigation Assistant (MANA) system is a broad project to assist elderly people, and those suffering from dementia or other ailments, with independent living in the privacy of their own home and the dignity of an ongoing personal life style.

3.1 MANA Calendar

The initial MANA Calendar application utilizes Head X to provide a talking head companion with an interface to Google Calendar, allowing doctors/carers to enter appointments/events that are provided to patients by the Head on a flexible reminder schedule. Eventually, it will provide localized assistance on how to get to the appointment based on public timetables, trip-planners and previous visits, but currently this information is supplied by carers.

The initial Calendar application of the MANA system was developed in 2009 based on preliminary input from an Alzheimer's Association for deployment in the homes of Alzheimer's sufferers. A preliminary exploration of potential faces and voices was conducted using a focus group approach organized through the NGO. For this preliminary stage we developed a dozen representative face/voice/script combinations and had representatives of the community select (individually and anonymously) their preferred face and voice. In associated discussion, it was apparent that a major influence was how authoritative the ECA appeared, and this was influenced by both face and voice (as well as the accent as their were only a couple of high quality voices available for each of the different accents). Some comments indicated that the person was too young or not serious enough, while positive comments were along the lines of that's matron, or an orderly, or that's someone authoritative – I'd do what they told me. At a later stage, if we have funds for a comprehensive study, it would be interesting to examine this formally, but for now we believe our "experts" and have developed our trial around the two most popular and authoritative male and female faces and voices. As a final stage, we dynamically combined and altered their preferred faces to achieve those characteristics preferred by the group.

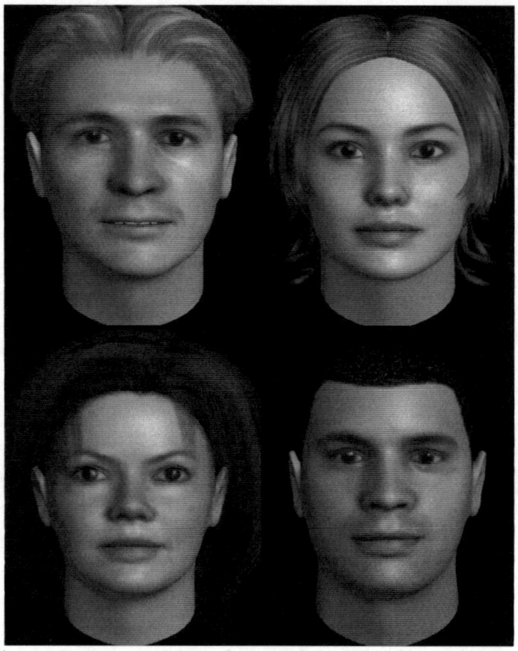
Figure 2. Four MANA faces selected by focus group.

These top four faces (Fig. 2) and the top four voices are those from which subjects are allowed to select the ECA for their trial. As our aim is to show the ECA in the best possible light, we aim to please and give the subject control over who it is they are inviting into their home – and they do seem to treat it as a person they are inviting.

The system comprises the following major components (Self-Reference,2010):

Web Calendar Appointment Interface: Essentially this interface works virtually identical to a standard Google calendar, where a doctor/carer can enter an appointment/event. The MANA Calendar then extracts the key aspects of the event (i.e: time, date, name, etc) and relays the information to the Calendar Manager.

Calendar Manager and Synapse Module: The central Calendar Manager converts the information into a coherent human-like message to be delivered by the Thinking Head, upon either a set reminder time or upon a person-event. As Synapse is used by system modules, intermodule communications ensure concurrent productions, e.g. the timing of voice audio and visemes (visual phonemes), appear as human-like as possible.

Thinking Head and SAPI/Mary Integration: This new Thinking Head was designed using FaceGen™ software and incorporates Mary and Nuance voices, giving greater flexibility than using the original Stelarc face and voice.

Face Detection and Motion Analysis Module: The system uses a camera which monitors the space the subject moves around in (or a part of it), and triggers upon detecting sufficient motion energy for a human body and a human face (using the algorithm of Viola & Jones (2004)). On detecting such a "person-event", the appointment message is then delivered to the subject.

Speech Recognition Trigger Module: At any time the subject can query the MANA Calendar system by uttering "MANA" and one of 3 key words "appointment" (for upcoming appointments), "date" (current date) or "time" (current time) subject to sufficiently low noise conditions. After making a timed announcement, the system enters a state in which the speech system is set to recognize several acknowledgements (like "OK").

MANA Calendar is being trialed in the homes of people with Alzheimer's disease during the first half of 2010. We require that there is at least one carer or health worker who is able to enter calendar information into Google Calendar for the primary subject. If we have a live in carer, or a spouse or relative in the carer role, we are also allowing them to enter their own appointments.

Currently we are using a multiuser Microsoft Speech Recognition system that is *not* trained to the specific user. For our (younger) voices tested pre-trial these gave pretty good results, but the system is sensitive to age and accent. We have therefore adapted the study to provide training opportunities (human and system) for those who cannot initially use the speech recognition system successfully.

In addition, we do have a back up mouse or switch arrangement that allows such a user to use the system, but we are not permitting use of this option at present. MANA Calendar is designed not to require use of either keyboard or mouse, and this is the condition that we are insisting on for our initial evaluation. MANA is meant to appear as a companion, not as a computer.

Another problem that we encountered is that the price point requested by the NGO was \$1000-\$1500, and for these experiments we are using a DELL Studio One which is really not quite fast enough for continuous speech. Thus if it is left on trying to follow a conversation, it ends up filling up its buffer which gives unacceptable response times. For this reason we not only require the user to say a specific keyword or name to get the attention of the system (by default, MANA), we also require the user to be looking at the ECA (Viola and Jones, 2004) before we try to interpret what they say as a command. This dramatically reduces the delays, although there is still a hiatus that is slightly longer than is comfortable (about two seconds rather than the desired one second). This problem does not appear when run on a more powerful machine.

3.2 Mobile Living

A straightforward extension to MANA Calendar is to implement it on a mobile phone. We are currently exploring a couple of options for both technologies and platforms, the latter possibilities include the iPhone, Windows Mobile and Google Android, each of which has its *pro's* and *con's*.

Already MANA Calendar has options to allow the carer/healthworker to enter directions, and eventually a library of directions will be built up so that commonly visited places/recurring events, will not need reentry of directions. With the Mobile extension, MANA can also popup with reminders, make use of GPS, and let people know when to get off the bus, etc. This naturally combines in with current directions in GPS navigation systems and aids, as well as systems for keeping track of the elderly.

3.3 Teaching/Training

There are also several extensions of MANA envisaged that make use of our Teaching ECA technology, including teaching social skills, providing personalized family oriented reminders, and bridges to other technologies.

We also aim to keep the client occupied and interested in current events, interacting with family and friends, and actively stimulated and mentally engaged. The selection and implementation of these specific task-oriented activities, as well as playing games or doing exercises, is not unique but is beyond the scope of this paper and will not be reviewed. Our focus here is the naturalness and appropriateness of interaction, and exemplifying the kind of task-directed interaction which is *not* beyond the scope of current ECA technology.

3.4 Companion Robots

One of the first news items on our technology described it as "Companion Robots", picking up very quickly on this potential, notwithstanding the crude Eliza-like interactions. Interestingly this comes round full circle to the kind of ethical questions about the use of computers that were raised in the mind of her creator by those who wanted to put her to work immediately (Weizenbaum, 1976). Weizenbaum argued that we shouldn't have computerized psychiatrists who didn't really understand their patients, even if they were using the same techniques the human experts employed. And the world agreed with him! What has changed?

In terms of ECA vs Eliza technology, not much – the dialogue for HeadX is based on Alice, who whilst not much different in many ways from Eliza, at least had origins that sought to provide her with visual connection to the world. The current versions of Alice, reflect AIML code that is very similar in principle to Eliza code, and don't reflect anything of the real world except through the medium of canned dialogue.

The issue of computer control is not limited to dialogue and the issue of competence – computer controlled trains and buses and planes have been shown to be more reliable than humans under specified conditions, but still tend to be under direct supervision. Computer-guided missiles are for better or worse under an even more removed level of control. Our homes are full of gadgets, and most of us spend more time interacting with a computer and/or watching television than interacting directly with a person.

So WE will leave the ethics to society to determine what it wants. In an age where more people will be retired than working within the next twenty to forty years in most western countries, a MANA-type companion looks to be more of a necessity than a desired outcome.

Anecdotally, from our discussions with the NGOs and their staff, those who have had a district nurse or social worker visiting on a regular basis, tend to be happier with a human visitor than some technological solution. But those who do not have someone visiting regularly are more apprehensive about having a stranger in the homes telling then what to do and sapping their independence, than they are having a technology that purports to do the same things, or mediates between them and a remote visitor who does not invade the privacy of their own home.

4 Conclusion: A Competent Companion

In summary, WE see the key issue as competence, and so will conclude by outlining our approach to building the competence of MANA as a companion, rather than a calendar.

Emotion, Affect and Attitude: As discussed, one of our main lines of research at present is exploring and expanding the range of expressions and emotions, developing an AV corpus of carefully elicited spontaneous natural emotions, and cross-evaluating versus acted/programmed expressions.

AV Speech Recognition/Synthesis: Currently we can control the expression of our avatar through markup that is based on human judgements about what particular morphs of the face appear to show, and which are hand tuned to someone's idiosyncratic idea of what a particular emotion or expression looks like – it is already reasonably effective, but as an initial step has not been properly evaluated, although our initial evaluation results have shown that at least some of the markup is effective, and that some is not (without separating out at this stage the influence of the text and the mark up). The flip side of displaying an ECA face is recognizing human faces and expressions. Similarly there is a much neglected auditory synthesis and recognition side that goes beyond phoneme and word. Our motto is "one person's noise is another person's signal" and our aim is for both speech and noise to simultaneously analyze and account for all individual differences, gender and age characteristics, emotion/affect/attitude and related human attributes, as well as explicit social and linguistic gestures and expressions, including rhythmic and tonal prosody.

Dialogue Management and Understanding: Dialogue management is a term WE don't like in the context of companiable systems – it derives from use as a database front end for ordering pizzas or taxis. It has a very limited concept of understanding related to the specific application, and Eliza or Alice type systems are perfectly capable of giving arbitrarily good results just by learning a greater range of template-response patterns. Our companionable MANA system is grounded in the home environment and is being trained to talk about and monitor and react to what is going on in the home. At the moment it is focused on body language and facial expression, and shares with the ASD system an aim to understand and react appropriately. The Alice substrate already has a reasonably comprehensive dictionary built in, but all it can do with that is define things – it can't actually productively use the knowledge. The Stelarc-Alice substrate also has at least three distinguishable personae built in – one who is male and a performance artist, one who is female and pretending to be human, and one who is neuter and surprised that you thought it should have that human characteristic. The latter two are an amalgam of hundreds of different programmer/user enhancements, whilst the Stelarc persona is the work of a single person and reflects his wry humour so that at times it does feel like you are talking to him. We are building in access to a full encyclopedia, and the ability to answer a wide variety of questions from each entry. But this also is superficial without the ability to learn and reason.

Learning and Reasoning: From a technological Artificial Intelligence perspective, our primary focus is learning. Children learn from the time they are born (actually probably more like from about three months before they are born) and their learning and play are very similar to the research and experimentation of a scientist. Piagetian Psycholinguistics, and Piaget's 20 plus books on specific aspects of child learning, development and reasoning, views learning and reasoning as developing hand in hand, with the little scientists developing new insights and deeper reasoning models, and thus enabling learning more about their world, society, culture and language. Learning to speak and understand language involves making noises and making the connection between the vocal tract/facial articulations/gestures and the heard sounds. Unsupervised learning using supervised techniques is possible using cross-modal training. Approaches from Computational Intelligence based on simple models from genetics, ant colonies and bee swarms, also provide mechanisms and analogies that help see how a system can continuously adapt and improve. Generalization and reasoning are part of this. Our ability to learn language is not independent of our ability to understand the world but an extension of it, and the constraints and nature of language are strongly influenced by the constraints and nature of the world. This also includes meta-reasoning: our reasoning about the consequences of our logic, decisions and behaviour.

References

Stevan Harnad (1992) The Turing test is not a trick: Turing indistinguishability is a scientific criterion. SIGART Bulletin 3(4) pp. 9 - 10.

David M W Powers (1998) The total Turing test and the Loebner prize, Proceedings of the Joint Conferences on New Methods in Language Processing and Computational Natural Language Learning, ACL, pp.279-280.

M. Schröder & J. Trouvain (2003). The German Text-to-Speech Synthesis System MARY: A Tool for Research, Development and Teaching. *International Journal of Speech Technology, 6, pp. 365-377.*

Stuart C Shapiro (1992) The Turing test and the economist. SIGART Bulletin 3(4) pp. 10-11.

Paul A. Viola and Michael J. Jones, 2004. Robust real-time face detection, International Journal of Computer Vision, vol. 57, pp. 137–154.

Joseph Weizenbaum (1966), ELIZA - a computer program for the study of natural language communication between man and machine, CACM 9 (1): 36–45

Joseph Weizenbaum (1976), Computer Power and Human Reason: From Judgment To Calculation, San Francisco: W. H. Freeman

Is a Companion a distinctive kind of relationship with a machine?

Yorick Wilks
Florida Institute of Human and Machine Cognition
ywilks@ihmc.us

Abstract

I start from a perspective close to that of the EC COMPANIONS project, and set out its aim to model a new kind of human-computer relationship based on long-term interaction, with some tasks involved although a Companion should not be *inherently* task-based, since there need be no stopping point to its conversation. Some demonstration of its functionality will be given but the main purpose here is an analysis of what it is people might want from such a relationship and what evidence we have for whatever we conclude. Is politeness important? Is an attempt at emotional sympathy important or achievable? Does a user want a consistent personality in a Companion or a variety of personalities? Should we be talking more in terms of a "cognitive prosthesis (or orthosis)?" ---something to extract, organize, and locate the user's knowledge or personal information---rather than attitudes?

1. Introduction

It is convenient to distinguish Companions from both (a) conversational internet agents that carry out specific tasks, such as the train and plane scheduling and ticket ordering speech dialogue applications back to the MIT ATIS systems (Zue et al., 1992), and also from (b) descendants of the early chatbots PARRY and ELIZA, the best of which compete annually in the Loebner competition (Loebner). These have essentially no memory or knowledge but are simple finite state response sets, although ELIZA had primitive "scripts" giving some context, and PARRY (Colby, 1971) had parameters like FEAR and ANGER that changed with the conversation and determined which reply was selected at a given point.

I take plausible distinguishing features of a Companion agent to be:

1) that it has no central or over-riding task and there is no point at which its conversation is complete or has to stop, although it may have some tasks it carries out in the course of conversation;
2) That it should be capable of a sustained discourse over a long-period, possibly ideally the whole life-time of its principal user;
3) It is essentially the Companion of a particular individual, its principal user, about whom it knows a great deal of personal knowledge, and whose interests it serves—it could, in principle, contain all the information associated with a whole life;
4) It establishes some form of relationship with that user, if that is appropriate, which would have aspects associated with the term "emotion", and shared initiative is essential;
5) It is not essentially an internet agent or interface, but since it will have to have access to the internet for information (including the whole-life information about its user—which could be public data like Facebook, or life information built up by the Companion over long periods of interaction with the user) and to act in the world, e.g. to reserve at a restaurant or call a doctor. But a Companion *need not* be a robot to act in the world in this way, and we may as well assume its internet agent status, with access to open internet knowledge sources.

Given this narrowing of focus in this paper, what questions then arise and what choices does that leave open? We now discuss some obvious questions that have arisen in the literature:

i) Emotion, politeness and affection

Cheepen and Monaghan (1997) presented results some thirteen years ago that customers of some automata, such as ATMs, are repelled by excessive politeness and endless repetitions of "thank you for using our service", because they know they are dealing with a machine and such feigned sincerity is inappropriate. This suggests that politeness is very much a matter of judgment in certain situations, just as it is with humans, where inappropriate politeness is often encountered. Wallis (Wallis et al., 2001) has reported results that many find computer conversationalists "chippy" or "cocky" and suggests that this should be avoided as it breeds hostility on the part of users; he believes this is always a major

Proceedings of the 2010 Workshop on Companionable Dialogue Systems, ACL 2010, pages 13–18,
Uppsala, Sweden, 15 July 2010.

risk in human-machine interactions.

We know, since the original work of Nass (Reeves and Nass, 1996) and colleagues that people will display some level of feeling for the simplest machines, even PCs in his original experiments, and Levy (2007) has argued persuasively that the trend seems to be towards high levels of "affectionate" relationships with machines in the next decades, as realistic hardware and sophisticated speech generation make machine interlocutors increasingly lifelike. However, much of this work is about human psychology, faced with entities known to be artificial, and does not bear directly on the issue of whether Companions should attempt to detect emotion in what they hear from us, or attempt to generate it in what they say back.

The AI area of "emotion and machines" is confused and contradictory: it has established itself as more than an eccentric minority taste, but as yet has nothing concrete to show beyond some better than random algorithms for detecting "sentiment" in incoming text (e.g. Wiebe et al., 2005), but even there its success is dependent on effective content extraction techniques. This work began as "content analysis" (Krippendorff, 2004) at the Harvard psychology department many years ago and, while prose texts may offer enough length to enable a measure of sentiment to be assessed, this is not always the case with short dialogue turns. That technology rested almost entirely on the supposed sentiment value of individual words, which ignores the fact that their value is content dependent. "Cancer" may be marked as negative word but the utterance "I have found a cure for cancer" is presumably positive and detecting the appropriate response to that utterance rests on the ability to do information extraction beyond single terms. Failure to observe this has led to many of the classic foolishnesses of chatbots such as congratulating people on the death of their relatives, and so on.

At deeper levels, there are conflicting theories of emotion for automata, not all of which are consistent and which apply only in limited ranges of discourse. So, for example, the classic theory that emotion is a response to the failure and success of the machine's plans (e.g. Marsella and Gratch, 2003) covers only those situations that are clearly plan driven and, as we noted, Companionship dialogue is not always closely related to plans and tasks. "Dimensional" theories (Cowie et al., 2001, following Wundt, 1913), display emotions along dimensions marked with opposed qualities (such as positive-negative) and normally distribute across the space emotion "primitives", such as FEAR, and these normally assigned by manual tagging. All such assignments of tags rest, like the text-sentiment theories above, on human pre-tagging. The problem with this is that tagging for "COMPANY" or "TEMPERATURE" (in classic NLP) is a quite different task from tagging for "FEAR" and "ANGER". These latter terms are not, and probably cannot be, analyzed but rest on the commonsense intuitions of the tagger, which may vary very much from person to person—they have very low consilience between taggers.

All this makes many emotion theories look primitive in terms of developments in AI and NLP elsewhere. Appraisal Theory (Scherer et al, 2008) seeks to explain why individuals can have quite different emotional reactions to similar situations because they have appraised them differently, e.g. a death welcomed or regretted. Appraisal can also be of the performance of planned activities, in which case this theory approximates to the plan-based one mentioned above. The theory itself, like all such theories, has a large-commonsense component, and the issue for computational implementation is how, in assessing the emotional state of the Companion's user to make such concepts quantitatively evaluable. If the Companion conducts long conversations with a user about his or her life, then one might expect there to be ample opportunity to assess the user's appraisal of, say, a funeral or wedding by means of the application of the sentiment extraction techniques to what is said in the presence of the relevant image. In so far as a Companion can be said to have over-arching goals, such as keeping the user happy then, to that degree, it is not difficult to envisage methods (again based on estimates of the happiness, or otherwise, of the user's utterances) for self-appraisal by the Companion of its own performance and some consequent causal link to generated demonstrations of its own emotions of satisfaction or guilt.

In speaking of "language" and Companions, we have so far ignored speech, although that is a communication mode in which a great deal has been done to identify and, more recently, generate, emotion-bearing components (Luneski et al., 2008). Elements of the above approaches can be found in the work of Worgan and Moore (see figure below, from REFERENCE REMOVED), where there is the same commitment to the centrality of emotion in the communication process, but in a form focusing on an integration of speech and language (rather than visual and design) technologies. Their argument is for a layer in a dialogue manager over and above local response management, but one which would seek to navigate the whole conversation across a two-dimensional space onto which Companion and user are mapped using continuous values (rather than discrete values corresponding to primitive but unexplained emotional terms) but in such a way as to both respond to the a user's demonstrated emotion appropriately, but also----again, if appropriate or chosen by the user----to draw the user back to other more positive emotional areas of the two-dimensional space. It is not yet clear what the right mechanism should be for the integration of this "landscape" global emotion-based dialogue manager should be with the local dialogue management that generates responses and alters the world context: in the Senior Companion this last was sophisticated stack of networks (see Wilks et al., in press). In some sense, we are just looking for a modern and defensible interface to replace what PARRY had in simple form in 1971 when the sum of two emotion parameters determined which response to select from a stack of alternatives.

This last is a high level issue to be settled in a Companion's architecture and also, perhaps, to be under the control of the user, namely: should a Companion invariably try to cheer a user up if miserable-----which is trying to "move" the user to the most naturally desirable (i.e. the top-right) quadrant of the space----or, rather, to track to the part of the space where the user is deemed to be and stay there in roughly the same emotional location—i.e. be sad with a sad user and happy with a happy one? There is no general answer to this question and, indeed, in an ideal Companion, which tracking method should be used would itself be a conversation topic e.g. "Do you want me to cheer you up or would you rather stay miserable?".

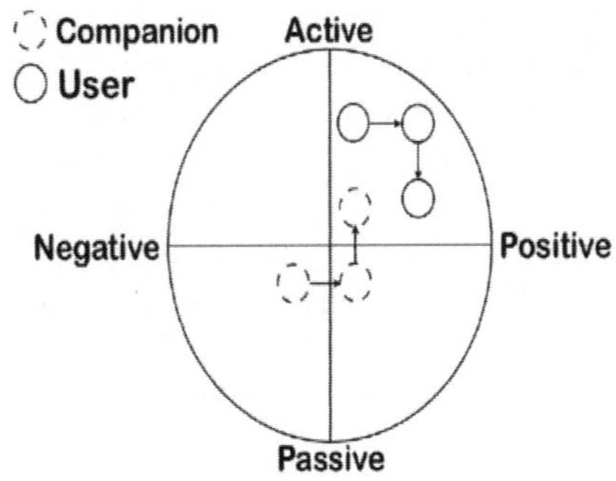

ii) What should a Companion look like?

A faceless Companion is a plausible candidate for Companionhood: the proverbial furry handbag, warm and light to carry, chatty but with full internet access. Such a Companion could always take control of a nearby screen or a phone if it needed to show anything. If there is to be a face, the question of the "uncanny valley effect" always comes up, where it is argued that users are more uneasy the more something is very like ourselves (Mori, 1970). But many observers do not feel this, and, indeed it cannot in principle apply to an avatar so good that one cannot be sure it is artificial, as many feel about the *Emily* from Manchester (Emily 2009).

On the other hand, if the quality is not good, and in particular if the lip synch is not perfect, it may be better to go for an abstract avatar ---the Companions logo was chosen with that in mind, and without a mouth at all. Non-human avatars seem to avoid some of the problems that arise with valleys and mixed feelings generally, and the best REMOVED demonstration video so far features REMOVED.

iii) Voice or Typing to communicate with a Companion?

At the moment the limitation on the use of voice is two-fold: first, although trained ASR for a single user—such as a Companion's user—is now very good and up in the high 90%, it still introduces uncertainty into understanding an utterance that is far greater than that of spelling errors. Secondly, it is currently not possible to store sufficient ASR software locally on a mobile phone to recognize a large vocabulary in real time; access to a remote server takes additional time and can be subject to fluctuations and delays. All of which suggests that a web-based Companion may have to use typed input in the immediate future—though using TTS output—

which is no problem for most mobile phone users, who have come to find typed chat perfectly natural. However, this is almost certainly only a transitory delay as mobile RAM increases rapidly and the problem should not determine research decisions---there is no doubt that voice will move back to the centre of communication once storage and access size have grown by another order of magnitude.

iv) One Companion personality or several?

Some (e.g. Pulman, in Wilks, 2010) have argued that having a consistent personality is a condition on Companionhood, but one could differ and argue that, although that is true of people—multiple personalities being a classic psychosis—there is no reason why we should expect this of a Companion. Perhaps a Companion should have a personality adapted to its particular relationship to a user at a given moment: Lowe (in Wilks, 2010) has pointed out that one might want a Companion to function as, say, a gym trainer, in which case a rather harsh attitude on the part of the Companion might well be the best one. If a Companion's emotional attitude were to (figuratively) move across a two dimensional emotion space (see diagram above) imitating or correcting what it perceived to be the user's state over time (as Worgan, see above, has proposed), then that shift in attitude might well seem to be the product of different personalities, as it sometimes can with humans.

It might be better, pace Pulman, to give a user access to, and some control over, the display of a multiple-personality Companion, something one could think of as an "agency" of Companions, rather than a single "agent", all of which shared access to the same knowledge of the world and of the state and history of the user.

v) Ethics and goals in the Companion

The issue is very close to the question of what goals a Companion can plausibly have, beyond something very general, such as "keep the user happy and do what they ask if you can", which are goals and constraints that directly relate to the standard discussions of the ethics a robot could be considered to have, a discussion started long ago by Asimov (1975). Clearly, there will be need for a Companion to have goals to carry out specific tasks: if it is to place a restaurant table booking on the phone for a user who has just said to it "Get me a table for two tonight at Branca around 8.30"---a phone request well within the bounds of the currently achievable technology-----and the Companion will first have to find the restaurant's phone number before it phones and ask about availability before choosing a reservation time. This is the standard content of goal-driven behavior, with alternatives at every stage if unexpected replies are encountered (such as the restaurant being fully booked tonight). But one does not need to consider such goals as "goals of its own" since they are inferred from what it was told and are simply assumed, as an agent or slave of the user. But a Companion that finds its user not responding after some minutes of conversation might well have to take an independent decision to call a doctor urgently, based on a stored permanent goal about danger to a user who is unable to answer but is not asleep etc.

vi) Safeguards for the information content of a Companion

Data protection, privacy, or whatever term one prefers, now captures a crucial concept in the new information society. A Companion that had learned intimate details of a user's life over months or years would certainly have contents needing protection, and many forces-----commercial, security, governmental, research---might well want access to it, or even to those of all the Companions in a given society. If societies move to a clear legal state where one's personal data is one's own, with the owner or originator having rights over sale and distribution of their data---which is not at all the case at the moment in most countries----then the issue of the personal data elicited by a Companion would automatically be covered.

If we ignore the issues of governments and national security---and a Companion would clearly be useful to the police when wanting to know as much as possible about a murder suspect, so that it might then be an issue of whether talking to one's Companion constituted any kind of self-incrimination, in countries where that form of communication is protected. Some might well want one's relationship to a Companion put on some basis like that of a relationship to a priest or doctor, or even to a spouse, who cannot always be forced to give evidence in common-law countries.

More realistically, a user might well want to protect parts of his or her Companion's information, or even an organized life-story based on that, from particular individuals: e.g. "this must never be told to my children, even when I am gone". It is not hard to imagine a Companion deciding whom to divulge certain things to, selecting between classes of offspring, relations, friends, colleagues etc. There will almost certainly need to be a new set of laws covering the ownership, inheritance and destruction of Companion-objects in the future.

vii) What must a Companion know?

There is no clear answer to this question: dogs make excellent Companions and know nothing. More relevantly, Colby's PARRY program, the best conversationalist of its day (Colby, 1971) and possibly since, famously "knew' nothing: John McCarthy at Stanford dismissed PARRY's performance by saying:"It doesn't even know who the US President is", forgetting as he said it that most of world's population did not know that, at least at the time. On the other hand, it is hard to relate over a long term to an interlocutor who knows little or nothing and has no memory of what it or you have said in the past. It is hard to attribute personality to an entity with no memory and little or no knowledge.

Much of what a Companion knows that is personal it should elicit in conversation from its user; yet much could also be gained from publicly available sources, just as the current Senior Companion demo goes off to Facebook, independently of a conversation, to find out who its user's friends are. Current information extraction technology (e.g. Ciravegna et al., 2004) allows a reasonable job to be made of going to Wikipedia for general information when, say, a world city is mentioned; the Companion can then glean something about that city from Wikipedia and ask a relevant question such as "Did you see the Eiffel Tower when you were in Paris?" which again gives a plausible illusion of general knowledge.

A concrete Companion paradigm: the Victorian Companion

The subsections above are mini-discussions of some of the constraints on what it is to be a Companion, the subject of a recent book collection (Wilks, 2010). The upshot of those discussions is that there are many dimensions of choice, even within an agreed definition of what a Companion is to be, and they will depend on the user's tastes and needs above all. In the section that follows, I cut though the choices and make a semi-serious proposal for a model Companion, one based on a once well-known social stereotype.

More seriously, and in the spirit of a priori thoughts (and what else can we have at this technological stage of development?) about what a Companion should be, I would suggest we could profitably spend a few moments reminding ourselves of the role of the Victorian lady's Companion. One could, and in no scientific manner, risk a listing of features of the ideal Victorian Companion:

1. Politeness
2. Discretion
3. Knowing their place
4. Dependence
5. Emotions firmly under control
6. Modesty
7. Wit
8. Cheerfulness
9. Well-informed
10. Diverting
11. Looks are irrelevant
12. Long-term relationship if possible
13. Trustworthy
14. Limited socialization between Companions permitted off-duty.

The Victorian virtue of discretion here brings to mind the "confidant" concept that Boden (in Wilks, 2010) explicitly rejected as being a plausible one for automated Companions:

Most secrets are secret from some HBs [Human Beings] but not others. If two CCs [Computer Companions] were to share their HB-users' secrets with each other, how would they know which other CCs (i.e. potentially, users) to 'trust' in this way? The HB could of course say "This is not to be told to Tommy"...... but usually we regard it as obvious that our confidant (sic) knows what should not be told to Tommy -- either to avoid upsetting Tommy, or to avoid upsetting the original HB. How is a CC to emulate that?

The HB could certainly say "Tell this to no-one" -- where "no-one" includes other CCs. But would the HB always remember to do that?

How could a secret-sharing CC deal with family feuds? Some family websites have special func-

tionalities to deal with this. E.g Robbie is never shown input posted by Billie. Could similar, or more subtle, functionalities be given to CCs?"

Boden brings up real difficulties in extending this notion to a computer Companion, but the problems are not all where she thinks. I see no difficulty in programming the notion of explicit secrets for a Companion, or even things to be kept from specific individuals ("Never tell this to Tommy"). Companions will have less problems remembering to be discrete than people do, and I suspect people have less instinctive discretion than Boden believes: they have to be told explicitly who to say what to, or not, in most cases, unless they are told to tell no one. In any case, much of this will be moot because Companions will normally deal only with one person except when, say, making phone calls to an official, friend or restaurant, where they can try to keep the conversation to limited replies that they can be sure to understand. The notion of a stored fact that must not be disclosed is relatively simple to code. Nonetheless, the Lady's Companion analogy foresees that Companions will, in time, gossip among themselves behind their owners' backs.

I would argue that the "Lady's Companion" list above an attractive and plausible one: it assumes emotion will be largely linguistic in expression, it implies care for the mental and emotional state of the user, and I would personally find it hard to abuse any computer with the characteristics listed above. Many of the situations discussed above are, at the moment, wildly speculative: that of a Companion acting as its owner's agent, on the phone or World Wide Web, perhaps holding power of attorney in case of an owner's incapacity and, with the owner's advance permission, perhaps even being a source of conversational comfort for relatives after the owner's death. Companions may not all be nice or even friendly: Companions to stop us falling asleep while driving may tell us jokes but will probably shout at us and make us do stretching exercises. Long-voyage Companions in space will be indispensable cognitive prostheses (or, more correctly, orthoses) for running a huge vessel and experiments above any beyond any personal services---Hollywood already knows all that.

Acknowledgement:

This work was funded by the Companions project sponsored by the European Commission as part of the Information Society Technologies (IST) programme under EC grant number IST-FP6-034434.

References

Colby, K.M. "Artificial Paranoia." Artif. Intell. 2(1) (1971), pp. 1-2

Cheepen, C. and Monaghan, J. 1997, 'Designing Naturalness in Automated Dialogues - some problems and solutions'. In Proceedings 'First International Workshop on Human- Computer Conversation', Bellagio, Italy.

Cowie, R., Douglas-Cowie, E., Tsapatsoulis, N., Votsis, G., Kollias, S., Fellenz, W. and Taylor, JG. 2001. Emotion recognition in human-computer interaction, Signal Processing Magazine, IEEE, 18(1), pp. 32–80.

Emily,2009.http://www.youtube.com/watch?v=UYgLFt5wfP4&feature=player_embedded#

http://www.surrealaward.com/avatar/3ddigital12.shtml

Krippendorff, K. 2004. Content Analysis: An Introduction to Its Methodology. 2nd edition, Thousand Oaks, CA: Sage.

Levy, D. 2007. Love and Sex with Robots: The Evolution of Human–Robot Relationships. London: Duckworth.

Luneski, A., Moore, R. K., & Bamidis, P. D. (2008). Affective computing and collaborative networks: towards emotion-aware interaction. In L. M. Camarinha-Matos & W. Picard (Eds.), Pervasive Collaborative Networks (Vol. 283, pp. 315-322). Boston: Springer.

Marsella, S. and Gratch, J. (2003) Modeling Coping Behavior in Virtual Humans: Don't Worry, Be Happy. 2nd Int Conf on Autonomous Agents and Multiagent Systems (AAMAS), Melbourne, Australia, July 2003.

Reeves, B., Nass, C. 1996, The media equation: how people treat computers, television, and new media like real people and places, Cambridge: Cambridge University Press, 1996.

Scherer, S., Schwenker, F. and Palm, G. 2008. Emotion recognition from speech using multi-classifier systems and rbf-ensembles, in Speech, Audio, Image and Biomedical Signal Processing using Neural Networks, pp. 49–70, Springer: Berlin.

Wallis, P., Mitchard, H., O'Dea, D., and Das J. 2001, Dialogue modelling for a conversational agent. In 'AI-2001: Advances in Artificial Intelligence', Stumptner, Corbett, and Brooks, (eds.), In Proceedings 14th Australian Joint Conference on Artificial Intelligence, Adelaide, Australia.

Wiebe, J., Wilson , T., and Cardie, C. 2005. Annotating expressions of opinions and emotions in language. Language Resources and Evaluation, volume 39, issue 2-3, pp. 165-210.

Wilks, Y. (ed.) (2010) Artificial Companions in Society: scientific, economic, psychological and philosophical perspectives. John Benjamins: Amsterdam.

Wundt, W., 1913. Grundriss der Psychologie, A. Kroner: Berlin.

Zue, V., Glass, J., Goddeau, D., Goodine, D., Hirschman, L. 1992. The MIT ATIS system, In Proc. Workshop on speech and natural language, Harriman, New York.

"Hello Emily, how are you today?" Personalised dialogue in a toy to engage children

Carole Adam
RMIT University
Melbourne, Australia.
carole.adam.rmit@gmail.com

Lawrence Cavedon
RMIT University
Melbourne, Australia.
lawrence.cavedon@rmit.edu.au

Lin Padgham
RMIT University
Melbourne, Australia.
lin.padgham@rmit.edu.au

Abstract

In line with the growing interest in conversational agents as *companions*, we are developing a toy companion for children that is capable of engaging interactions and of developing a long-term relationship with them, and is extensible so as to evolve with them. In this paper, we investigate the importance of personalising interaction both for engagement and for long-term relationship development. In particular, we propose a framework for representing, gathering and using personal knowledge about the child during dialogue interaction. [1]

1 Introduction

In recent years there has been an increasing interest in so-called *Companion* agents: agents that are intelligent, and built to interact naturally (via speech and other modalities) with their user over a prolonged period of time, personalising the interaction to them and developing a relationship with them. The EU Companions project[2] is the most well known such project, with applications such as a companion for the elderly (Field et al., 2009), and a health and fitness companion (Stahl et al., 2009). In our work, together with industry partners, we are developing a speech-enabled companion toy for children. While there are many "smart toys" on the market, as far as we are aware our work is unique in attempting to develop a "companion toy" for a child, evolving with them over a long period of time. As with other projects on intelligent companions, a crucial task is to build a long-term relationship with the user, by a series of interactions over time, that the user experiences as engaging and valuable.

According to models of the "enjoyability" of human-computer interaction (Brandtzaeg et al., 2006), there are three main features making an interactive system engaging for the user: the user should feel in **control** of the interaction (which includes being able to customise it and getting timely feedback); the **demands** on the user should be adapted to their capabilities, *i.e.* the interaction should be challenging and surprising but not overwhelming; and the system should **support** social interaction rather than isolating the user. Another important aspect of any engaging interaction is for it to be **personalised**, *i.e.* customised to the particular interlocutor and their environment. Other important features for engagement include coherence of the dialogue, emotional management, and personality. In this paper we focus specifically on the issue of appropriate personalisation of interactions with a child, and how to realise this.

Existing personalised systems mainly have a *task-oriented* focus, *i.e.* they aim at building a user profile and using it to facilitate the user's task (*e.g.* Web navigation assistants or product recommendation systems (Abbattista et al., 2003)), and at being user-configurable. On the contrary we aim at personalising the interaction to build a relationship and engage a child. The main novelties of our system are that: it is *not* task-oriented; it is specifically designed for children; and its behaviour is derived from actual interaction data. Indeed, in order to understand the kinds of personalisation occurring in natural dialogues with children, we have analysed corpora of children's dialogues (MacWhinney, 1995; MacWhinney, 2000). We have then developed a framework that enables the implementation of a number of these personalised behaviours within our intelligent toy.

The contribution of this paper is the **identification** of different kinds of personalisation behaviours in dialogue with children, based on actual data, plus the **framework** to realise these within an implemented system.

[1]A slightly longer version of this paper is currently under review elsewhere. If both papers are accepted for publication we will modify to ensure that they expand different aspects.

[2]See www.companions-project.org.

Proceedings of the 2010 Workshop on Companionable Dialogue Systems, ACL 2010, pages 19–24,
Uppsala, Sweden, 15 July 2010.

2 Personalisation behaviours

2.1 Corpus analysis

We have analysed examples of children-adult dialogues (mainly from the CHILDES database (MacWhinney, 1995; MacWhinney, 2000); one dialogue from a forthcoming study performed with a puppet as part of this project) in order to determine the types of behaviours that adults use to personalise their interaction with a child.

Relation to self

A first observation is that children often try to relate conversation to themselves. This is illustrated by this conversation between a girl (G) and her mother (M) about a visit to the doctor.

G *What's polio?*
M *An illness that makes you crippled. That's why you get all those injections and... A long time ago, kiddies, kiddies used to die with all that things.*
G *will I ?*
M *hmm. You aren't going to die.*

Personal questions

Adults also often ask the child questions about themselves. This dialogue illustrates a conversation between an adult (A) and a child (C) about C's holidays. Notice that the questions are adapted to the context (ask about holidays in summer).

A *Did you go on vacation over the summer? Did you?*
A *Where'd you go? To the beach?*
C *Yes.*
A *Yeah? Did you go by yourself? No. Why laugh? You could go by yourself.*
A *Do you have brothers and sisters?*
C *Just a little sister.*
A *A sister? Did she go too? On vacation?*

Child control

Even if the adult is asking the questions, the child retains some control over the interaction. The following dialogue between a boy (B) and his grandmother (G) shows how the adult follows the child when he switches away from a disliked topic. This dialogue also shows the adult commenting on the child's tastes based on her knowledge of them.

G *how are you getting on in school?*
B *we're not going to go shopping today.*
G *eh?*
B *shopping today.*
G *...*
B *and chips.*
G *going to have chips?*
B *mm.*
G *you likes that.*

Reciprocity

Another way for the adult to learn personal information about the child without asking questions is to confide personal information first, which encourages the child to reciprocate. In this dialogue between a child (C) and a puppet (P) controlled by an adult, P confides personal information (its tastes), which leads the child to do the same.

P *My favourite drink is lemon. Lemon soft drink. I like that.*
C *Mine is orange juice.*
P *mmhm. Orange one? You like the orange one?*
C *Orange juice (*nodding*)*

Recalling shared activities

Another form of personalisation is recalling past shared activities. In the following dialogue, a mother (M) reads a book to her child (C); when a picture of a snowman appears in the book she recalls the child recently making one with her.

M *what did we make outside here today?*
C *um I don't know.*
M *did we make a man?*
C *yeah.*
M *a snowman?*
C *yeah.*

Child's preferences

Another way to personalise interaction is to recall a child's preferences. For example this dialogue involves a child (C) and an interrogator (I) wanting to record a story. Here the child corrects incorrect knowledge; this update should be remembered.

I *Do you wanna tell a story?*
C *No. I won't.*
I *No, you don't.*
I *You told me down there that you like stories.*
C *No, I hate stories.*

Child's agenda

Parents may also use knowledge about a child's agenda (*i.e.* planned future activities, school, etc.) and make relevant and timely comments about it. In this dialogue a mother (M) and her friend (F) talk with a boy (B) about his next school day, when he is supposed to see chicken eggs hatching.

F *Oh you're going to see the little chicks tomorrow are you. You'll have to tell me what it's like. I haven't never seen any.*
B *I I haven't either.*
F *I haven't.*
M *We've seen them on the tellie, haven't we?*
F *I haven't seen those little ones.*
M *haven't you?*
F *So you'll have to tell me.*
M *Have you seen them on the tellie?*
B *mm [= yes].*

We notice again that when the mother's friend confides some information (she never saw that), the child reciprocates (he neither). Moreover the mother again shows memory of past activities (seeing something on television).

2.2 Personalisation strategies

Based on our analysis of adult-children dialogue corpora, we have designed a number of strategies to allow our toy to generate these kinds of personalised interactions with the child. These strategies fit into two categories: strategies for **gathering** personal information, and strategies for **exploiting** personal information.

Information gathering

The Toy can gather and then use different types of information: (1) personal information (e.g. family, friends, pets); (2) preferences (e.g. favourite movie, favourite food); (3) agenda (plays football on Saturday, has maths every Thursday); (4) activity-specific information (preferred stories, current level of quiz difficulty); (5) interaction environment (e.g. time, day, season, weather).

The easiest strategy to gather this information is to explicitly query the child. These queries have to be made opportunistically, *e.g.* when matching the current conversational topic, so as to seamlessly integrate information gathering into a conversation. Other strategies include confiding personal information to make the child reciprocate and confide similar information; or extracting personal information from spontaneous child's input. These strategies are useful so as to avoid asking too many questions, which would dirupt the conversation flow and could annoy the child.

Information exploitation

One of the challenges for using the gathered personal information in a conversation is to determine the appropriate opportunities to do so. The personal information can be used to engage the child in various ways, reproducing the types of behaviours illustrated above. In particular, our toy has the following information exploiting strategies: (1) use child's name; (2) insert comments using personal information; (3) ask about daily activities; (4) adapt interaction (*e.g.* greetings) to the context (*e.g.* time of day); (5) take child's preferences into account in topic or activity selection.

3 The Toy architecture: overview

This section outlines the general architecture of the toy. The integration of our personalisation framework is detailed in Section 4.

The central component of the Toy is the *Dialogue Manager* (DM) which is made up of two components: the *input/output manager* (IOM) receives input from Automatic Speech Recognition (ASR)[3] and sends output to Text-to-Speech (TTS); the *Semantic Interaction Manager* (SIM) receives input from IOM, generates the toy's response and sends it back to IOM (see Figure 1).

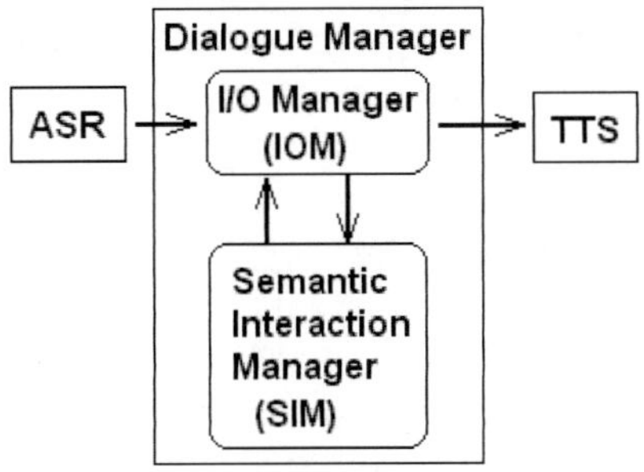

Figure 1: Architecture of the Toy

Our current approach to ASR and utterance processing is grammar-based: on sending an output utterance for synthesis, the DM loads into the speech recogniser a parameterised grammar specifying the set of expected user responses to this output. The DM is multi-domain and extensible via *domain modules*, designed to handle utterances about a particular domain, and encapsulating data required for this: a knowledge-base segment; a set of *conversational fragments* (see Section 3.2.2); a collection of the *topics* it is designed to handle; and an entry grammar to assign a topic to inputs.

3.1 Input Output Manager

The IOM is implemented using a BDI agent-oriented methodology, with dialogue processing "strategies" built as plans. For example, there are plans designed to handle errors or low-confidence results from speech recognition; plans to handle utterance content and update the information state; and plans to manage concurrent conversational threads and select which of a number of candidate responses to output.

3.2 Semantic Interaction Manager

The Semantic Interaction Manager (SIM) is a component designed to manage flexible conversational flow. The SIM maintains an *agenda* of things to say. When an input is received from the IOM, it is pre-processed to generate an input analysis that informs the further stages of the

[3] We have mainly used SRI's *Dynaspeak* system which is designed for small computational platforms.

SIM plan. In particular the input is then either dispatched to an existing ongoing *activity* if it matches its expected answers, or an appropriate new activity is created. The chosen activity selects a *conversational fragment* in the topic network corresponding to its topic, and writes it in the conversational agenda. Finally the output is generated from the agenda and sent to the IOM.

3.2.1 The conversational agenda

The conversational agenda maintained by the SIM has two main parts. The *history* represents the past interaction and stores past *questions under discussion* (QUD) (Ginzburg, 1997) with their received answer. The *stack* represents the future interaction and lists QUD to be asked next, in order. The agenda also stores the current ongoing activities (Section 3.2.3), making it possible to switch back and forth between them.

3.2.2 Conversational fragments

In our system, we use pre-scripted pieces of dialogue that we call *conversational fragments*. The designers of domain modules will provide a *topic network* describing its domain, with nodes being the possible topics, having links with other topics, and providing a pool of fragments to possibly use when talking about this topic. Each fragment has an applicability condition, and provides the text of an output as well as a list of expected answer patterns with associated processing (*e.g.* giving feedback) applied when the child's response matches.

This representation obviates the need for full natural language generation (NLG) by providing semi-scripted outputs, and also informs the grammar-based ASR by providing a list of expected child answers. Moreover it allows the Toy to generate quite flexible interactions by switching between topics and using fragments in any order.

3.2.3 Activities

When interacting with the child, the Toy suggests possible *activities* (*e.g.* quiz, story) about the available topics. Each type of activity uses specific types of fragments (*e.g.* quiz questions with expected (in)correct answers; story steps with expected questions) and has particular success and failure conditions (*e.g.* a number of (in)correct answers for a quiz; or reaching the end for a story).

This concept of activity helps to keep the dialogue cohesive, while allowing flexibility. It also meets the requirement that an engaging interaction should be *demanding* for the child while staying *controlled* by them. Indeed a number of activities can be listed in the agenda at the same time, being resumed or paused to allow switching between them (*e.g.* to follow the child's topic requests or to insert personalised contributions).

4 The toy personalisation framework

We now describe our framework for implementing the personalisation strategies specified earlier.

4.1 The personalisation frame

All the information that our toy needs to personalise an interaction is gathered using a structure called the *personalisation frame*. This structure is tailored to the requirements imposed by our architecture, namely the grammar-based speech recognition and the absence of natural language processing. It consists of: (1) a static list of personal information **fields** (*e.g.* child name, age); (2) a static indexed list of **rules** specifying when it is appropriate to insert personal comments or questions in the interaction; (3) a dynamic child **profile**, storing the current values of (some) personal information fields, updated during interaction.

Personal information fields (PIFs)

Each personal information field contains: a list of possible values for this field (informing the ASR grammar); and a grammar of specific ways in which the child may spontaneously provide information relevant to this field (allowing the toy to interpret such input and extract the value).

For example the field "favourite animal" has a list of animals as its values, and its grammar contains patterns such as "My favourite animal is X" or "I love X" (where the variable X ranges over the possible values of this field).

Personalisation rules

Each personalisation rule specifies the opportunity that triggers it, and the text of the output. The text of personalisation comments and questions is scripted, and used to automatically generate conversation fragments from the frame. **Comment rules** also specify the list of personal information fields that are used in the text of the comment, while **Question rules** specify the name of the field set by their answer and a grammar of expected answers, with their interpretation in terms of which value the corresponding field should receive.

For example, there may be a *comment rule* referring to the field *pet_type*, enabling the output "I know you have a *pet_type*" when the keyword *pet_type* is detected. There may also be a *question rule* for asking "What is your favourite animal?" when talking about the zoo; expected answers would include "I like *A*"; so if the child answers "I like tigers" then the *favourite_animal* field would receive the value "tigers" as a result.

Opportunities

Personalisation must be integrated into the conversational management so as not to disrupt dialogue (*i.e.* the toy should still maintain a coherent interaction). It is thus important to accurately detect appropriate opportunities to insert personalisation side-talk. There are three types of opportunities that can trigger the personalisation rules: (1) **keyword opportunities** (a particular keyword appears in the child's input, *e.g.* the child uses the word "mother"); (2) **topic opportunities** (the interaction is focused on a particular topic, *e.g.* the child is talking about koalas); (3) **activity opportunities** (a particular activity is in a particular state, *e.g.* start of a story).

The following sections describe how this *personalisation frame* is used in the Conversation Manager process to personalise the conversation that is generated: we first outline the full process, before giving details about the steps where the *personalisation frame* is used.

4.2 Personalised input handling

The following algorithm is the result of the integration of personalisation into the response generation plan of the SIM. Steps manipulating the personalisation frame will be detailed below.

```
 1. Initialisation (load child profile,
    update environment description);
 2. Input reception (from IOM):
 3. Input analysis (preprocess input,
    detect opportunities);
 4. Profile update;
 5. Input dispatching (to selected
    activity);
 6. Activity progressing (fragment
    selection);
 7. Personalisation generation (generate
    fragment from best applicable
    triggered rule);
 8. Agenda processing (prioritisation
    of activity vs personalisation
    fragments);
 9. Personalisation of output (detection
    of opportunities, modification of
    output);
10. Output generation (sent to IOM);
11. End turn (save profile).
```

Fragment selection (step 6)

Fragment selection is personalised in two ways. **First**, some fragments have applicability conditions concerning the interaction context and the child's profile. For example a fragment such as "Hi, what's your name?" is only applicable if the toy does not know the child's name. A greeting fragment such as "Hi! How was school today?" is only applicable at the end of a school day. Other greeting fragments are available for different contexts. **Second**, some fragments have an adaptable content, using variables referring to the child's profile and to the context. These fragments are only applicable if the value of these variables is known and can be used to instantiate the variable when generating output. For example a fragment with the text "Hello *child_name*! How are you?" is applicable once the child's name is known. Or a fragment saying "I know you have a *pet_type* called *pet_name*." will be instantiated as "I know you have a cat called Simba".

Personalisation fragments generation (step 7)

When an opportunistic rule in the personalisation frame is triggered, its applicability is checked: *comment rules* are only applicable if the fields used have a value; *question rules* are only applicable if the field set has no value. Then the applicable rule of highest priority is used to generate a personalisation fragment. Its topic is the current topic provided in the input analysis; its type is either "personal question" or "personal comment"; and its text is as specified in the rule. Comment fragments have no additional applicability condition and no expected answers. Question fragments receive the generic expected answers specified in the rule, instantiated with the possible values of the field set by this question; the process associated with them consists in setting the value of this field to the value extracted from the input; the default process stores the full input as the value.

For example with the *question rule* "What is your favourite animal?" shown above, the generated fragment will expect answers such as "I like tigers", "I like giraffes", *etc.* If a matching answer is received, then the corresponding animal is stored as the child's favourite one in their profile.

Prioritisation (step 8)

When updating the agenda, several situations can arise depending on the relative priorities of personalising the interaction vs continuing the current activity. If the activity can be disrupted at this point, personalisation question fragments can be added on top of the stack in the agenda, while comments can be appended to the activity output; if the personalisation fragment has too low priority to disrupt the activity, then it is dropped. This priority of personalisation depends in particular on the priority of the triggered rule and on the time since personalisation was last inserted.

5 Conclusion

This framework for personalisation has been implemented in our toy using the Java-based agent platform Gorite (Ronnquist, 2008). The following is an example of the type of dialogues we intend to generate with it (T is the Toy and C a child); it illustrates a number of our personalisation strategies. Our infrastructure technically allows it to happen, however we still need to add more content (domain modules and fragments in them) to make it actually happen; we are working on writing such content, as well as on providing tools to make it easier for designers to write this content in the future.

C *Hi there*
T *Hello Emily!* `[Use child's name]`
T *What did you do on such a sunny week-end?* `[Context-adaptation]`
C *I went to the zoo!*
T *Great! That must have been fun. Which animals did you see?*
C *I saw tigers*
T *Tigers are cats, but much bigger than your cat Simba. What else did you see?*
C *Koalas!*
T *Oh, that's your favourite animal, isn't it?* `[Personal comment]`
C *Yes*
T *You must have been really happy. My favourite animal is orangutan, did you see any?* `[Confide personal information]`
C *No*
T *Pity... Allright, enough chatting. I know you love stories. Do you want to hear a story about tigers?* `[Choose favourite activity]`

The ASR is not functional yet due to the specific challenges of recognizing children voices, so for now we are only experimenting with a textual interface. This may look similar to a *chatbot* but has additional functionalities such as playing activities, and maintaining a context of interaction, including the history of the past interaction (in order not to repeat itself), physical context (to tailor interaction to the date, time, weather...), and a profile of the user (to personalise interaction to them). Contrarily to a chatbot which is designed for short-term interactions, we expect such a *companion* agent to be able to develop a long-term relationship with the user. This will be tested with a Wizard of Oz setting before our industrial partner provides us with a children-specific ASR.

The dialogue above is obviously not as rich as child-mother interactions from the CHILDES corpus; in particular it lacks the recognition of emotions and expression of empathy that is essential in human interactions. Therefore future directions for research include detecting the child's emotions (we have been experimenting with OpenEar (Eyben et al., 2009) to detect emotions from voice); reasoning about detected emotions, using an existing BDI model of emotions (Adam, 2007); helping the child to cope with them, in particular by showing empathy; and endowing the toy with its own personality (Goldberg, 1993).

6 Acknowledgements

This project is supported by the Australian Research Council, and RealThing Pty Ltd. under Linkage Grant LP0882013

References

F. Abbattista, G. Catucci, M. Degemmis, P. Lops, G. Semeraro, and F. Zambetta. 2003. A framework for the development of personalized agents. In *KES*.

C. Adam. 2007. *Emotions: from psychological theories to logical formalisation and implementation in a BDI agent*. Ph.D. thesis, INP Toulouse, France.

P. B. Brandtzaeg, A. Folstad, and J. Heim. 2006. Enjoyment: Lessons from karasek. In M. A. Blythe, K. Overbeeke, A. F. Monk, and P. C. Wright, editors, *Funology: From Usability to Enjoyment*. Springer.

F. Eyben, M. Wollmer, and B. Schuller. 2009. openEAR: Introducing the Munich open-source emotion and affect recognition toolkit. In *ACII*, Amsterdam.

D. Field, R. Catizone, W. Cheng, A. Dingli, S. Worgan, L. Ye, and Y. Wilks. 2009. The senior companion: a semantic web dialogue system. (demo). In *AAMAS*.

J. Ginzburg. 1997. Resolving questions I and II. *Linguistics and Philosophy*, 17 and 18.

L. R. Goldberg. 1993. The structure of phenotypic personality traits. *American Psychologist*, 48:26–34.

B. MacWhinney. 1995. *The CHILDES Database*.

B. MacWhinney. 2000. *The CHILDES project: Tools for analyzing talk*. Lawrence Erlbaum Associates.

R. Ronnquist. 2008. The goal oriented teams (gorite) framework. In *Programming Multi-Agent Systems*, volume LNCS 4908, pages 27–41. Springer.

O. Stahl, B. Gamback, M. Turunen, and J. Hakulinen. 2009. A mobile health and fitness companion demonstrator. In *EACL*.

A Robot in the Kitchen

Peter Wallis,
Department of Computer Science
The University of Sheffield
Sheffield, S1 4DP, UK
p.wallis@dcs.shef.ac.uk

Abstract

A technology demonstrator is one thing but having people use a technology is another, and the result reported here is that people often ignore our lovingly crafted handiwork. The SERA project - Social Engagement with Robots and Agents - was set up to look explicitly at what happens when a robot companion is put in someone's home. Even if things worked perfectly, there are times when a companion's human is simply not engaged. As a result we have separated our "dialog manager" into two parts: the dialog manager itself that determines what to say next, and an "interaction manager" that determines when to say it. This paper details the design of this SALT-E architecture.

1 Introduction

The SERA project, funded under FP7-ICT call 3, was initially intended to take established technology and put it in people's homes so we could record what happens. The core idea was to provide data in order to compare alternate methodologies for moving from raw data to the next generation of synthetic companion. Our primary motivation for the proposal was the realisation that the semantics of language is just one part of language in use. Even in apparently task based dialogs, effective repair strategies are essential and, what is more, highly dependent on social skills. Although there are many ways of looking at language, do any of them provide the kind of information, and level of detail, required to build better conversational agents?

The focus has turned out to be on robots rather than embodied conversational agents and the robot of choice was a Nabaztag. The Nabaztag is a commercially produced talking head from Violet in the style of Kismet and the Philips iCat. It is a stylized rabbit with expressive ears, a set of multi colour LEDs and is marketed as the world's first internet enabled talking rabbit. The rabbit connects to the Violet server via a wireless router and can run several applications including receiving SMS messages, weather reports, tai chi, and streaming selected radio or blog sites.

Figure 1: Making an omelette. In the real world, people ignore our handiwork! (note Nabaztag ears in the foreground)

The target participant group for the SERA experiments was older people with little experience of the limitations of computers. As it turns out, our subjects to date all have personal computers at home, but the lack of a keyboard or screen, and the rabbit being the only visible "beige-ware" means the set-up has been seen as sufficiently novel to provide classic discourse behaviour in spite of its limitations.

The original scenario was to have the rabbit provide classic internet services but our connection with the National Health Service (UK) through one of the participants provided impetus for us to use a health related theme and enabled us to recruit some interesting people through Help the

Proceedings of the 2010 Workshop on Companionable Dialogue Systems, ACL 2010, pages 25–30,
Uppsala, Sweden, 15 July 2010. ©2010 Association for Computational Linguistics

Aged (Hel, 2010), Aged Concern (Age, 2010) and similar organisations.

The primary result so far is that the established technology is seriously wanting. Our initial intention was to put a Nabaztag in people's homes pretty much as it comes out of the box. The problem is that these robots are intended to be entertaining rather than useful and the novelty soon wears off. As Mival et al point out (Mival et al., 2004) it is quite a challenge to design something that doesn't "end up in the back of the cupboard with the batteries out." Indeed these machines are expected to be on a desk, and to be poked and prodded to make them do things. For instance, the messaging function of the Nabaztag is certainly fun and useful, but there are two modes in its standard format: in the first the rabbit gives the message and assumes you are there. There is no sensing of the environment; the rabbit simply blurts it out. In the second mode it acts more like a classic answering machine and the user is expected to press a button to prompt a conversation about messages. Although this might be useful, it is acting exactly like a classic answering machine and we thought we could do significantly better by adding a PIR sensor - a standard home security passive infra red sensor that detects movement. We thus skipped the first version of our set-up and moved straight to a slightly more pro-active version that incorporated a PIR sensor to detect if the user was present. This is where the trouble starts, and is the primary point addressed in this paper.

The second piece of wanting technology is ASR — the automatic speech recognition. We initially considered a range of possibilities for the ASR and settled on Dragon Naturally Speaking, version 10 (DNS). In part this was driven by the fact that other projects were using it, and in part because of the DNS reputation. If we had gone for something else and it didn't work, well, people would have asked why we didn't use DNS. As it turned out, we could not get DNS to work with our set-up and for the first pass we resorted to yes/no buttons. Despite failing to get it working, using DNS was probably the right decision for exactly the reason given above. For the effort to have any impact however, other researchers need to know what happened and to this end the next section details our woes.

2 Speech Recognition

Speech recognition has been seen as "almost there" for twenty years and, from Furbys to interactive voice response phone systems, there are instances where the technology is useful. What is more, there is a body of work that points to the word recognition rates being less critical than one might assume (Wallis et al., 2001; Skantze, 2007). We allocated three months of a speech post-doc to get something working and expected it to take a week. We considered several options including DNS, Loquendo's VoxNauta which has a garbage model (see below) the Sphinx-4 system from CMU which is open source and in Java, the Juicer system (Moore et al., 2006) for which we have local expertise, and the ubiquitous HTK ToolKit which would certainly have the flexibility to do what we thought needed doing but would, no doubt, result in something cobbled together and unreliable. On the plus side we did have a single user that we could train but on the minus, we felt a head-set microphone was out of the question for the type of casual interaction we were expecting.

From the outset the intention was to use word spotting in continuous speech rather than attempting to parse the user's input. This was primarily motivated by the observation that successful NLP technologies such as chatbots and information extraction work that way. What is more, unlike dictating a letter or capturing an academic talk, we expected our subjects would not talk in full sentences, and utterances to be quite short. A command based system was considered but we did not want to restrict it to "Say yes, or no, now" style dialogs.

The approach we took was to use DNS as a large vocabulary continuous speech recognizer and then run regex style phrase spotting over the result - a classic pipeline model. The architecture was, and remains, an event driven model in which the dialog manager unloads and loads sets of "words of interest" into the recognizer at pretty well each turn. These sets are of phrases rather than words, and ideally would include the regex equivalent of ".+" and "" - that is "anything said" and "nothing said". The recognizer then reports back whenever something of interest occurs in the input, and does it in a timely manner.

The motivation for integrating speech and language this closely is the belief that the dialog manager can have a quite concise view of what the subject will say next. What is more, getting it wrong is not critical if (and only if) the dialog manager has a decent repair strategy. The first of these beliefs is discussed further below, and the second is based on the results such as those in Wallis and in Skantze mentioned above.

The result was that we failed to get speech recognition working for the first iteration - despite the world leading expertise in the group. To quote from the 12 month project review:

> The COTS speech recognition did not prove as effective as supposed in the unstructured domestic environment, partly because of poor accuracy but also because of unacceptable latency imposed by the language model. Effective ASR deployment was further complicated by lack of access to the workings of the underlying proprietary recognition engine. ... and there is now a wider realisation and acceptance among partners that ASR is not a solved problem. [sera m12 review, 25/03/2010]

It turns out that a significant part of the performance delivered from dictation systems comes from the language model, not from the sound itself. The result was firstly that the system would wait for more input when the user didn't produce a grammatical sentence. This latency was often well beyond the point at which the resulting silence is treated by the user as information bearing. Secondly, when we did grab the available parts of the decision lattice in order to fix the latency issue, the hypotheses were very poor. Presumably this is because the language model was providing evidence based on the false assumption that the user would speak in proper sentences. Trials are under way to test this. The take away message is that dictation systems are not necessarily suited to interactive dialog. We have since heard that there are "secret switches" that those in the know can adjust (Hieronymus, 2009) on DNS but, in retrospect, if one is forced to use a COTS product one might be better off using a system such as VoxNauta that acknowledges the needs of interactive systems by including a garbage model. At least Loquendo have thought about the problems of interactive speech even if there is an apparent performance difference as measured in terms of word error rates.

The extent to which ASR relies on the language model encourages us further to believe that a tightly coupled dialog manager and speech recognition system will prove significantly better than simply piping data from one module to another.

3 Situated agents

If you use a chatbot, or trial a demo, you necessarily attend to the artifact. Your attention is on it, you want your attention on it, and the trial satisfactorily ends when you stop attending to it. Alarms are designed to demand attention, but what should a companion do? Figure 1 is a typical scene in participant number one's kitchen. She is making an omelette, and has told the rabbit that she is making an omelette. Now she is not attending to the rabbit and so what should the rabbit do? In particular, the rabbit can receive SMS style messages and if one arrives as she is making her omelette, should the rabbit pass it on now or wait until the next time she talks to it? There is of course no right answer to this but the issue does need to be managed. This is not a problem for a demo in which the action is scripted, and it is not an issue for the Nabaztag in its commercial form as it only knows when a message arrives, and when the user presses the button. With a PIR sensor however the system knows that someone is there, but are they paying attention? In the first iteration the system was cobbled together with a quite linear approach to system initiative. The latest version takes a slightly more sophisticated approach and distinguishes between three states at the top level. The system is:

- Sleeping – not seeing or hearing anything,
- Alert – "attending to" the person,
- Engaged - it is committed a conversation

The most obvious case of engagement is when the person and the machine are having a conversation - that is Listening and Talking to each other, however even if the conversation is finished, the system may still want to keep the context of the recent discussion. As an example the system might have finished its (system initiated) conversation about the day ahead and wait to see if the human wants to talk about their day before moving back to the Alert state in which the subject would need to go through the process of initiating a discussion.

These four states, Sleeping, Alert, Talking, or Listening (Engaged) are controlled by external

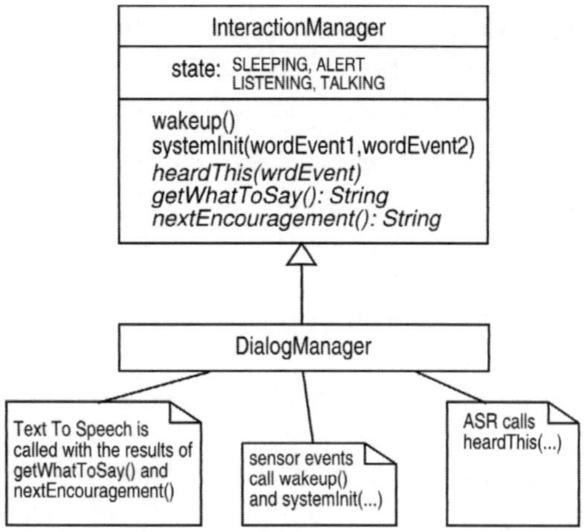

Figure 2: The InteractionManager handles *when* to say somethng; the DialogManager *what* to say.

events and timers. The GUI for editing dialog action frames provides 4 timing values as follows:

- Pause 1 indicates the end of a turn by the user - it is an opportunity for the system to say something.
- Pause 2 indicates the system ought to say something, and with nothing to say, it does an encouragement.
- Pause 3 is the time after which the system drops the context of the conversation.
- Pause 4 is the time at which the system goes to Sleep after the last PIR event.

Mapping these pauses into action, at pause 1 the system may move from Listening to Talking; pause 2 is the same but with a conversational "filler". At pause 3 it moves from Engaged to Alert, and pause 4 from Alert to Sleeping. The PIR sensor is the primary means by which the system is moved from Sleeping to Alert, and Alert to Engaged (actually Listening) can be human initiated by calling the system by name - "Hey Furby!" being used on that classic toy, and "Computer" being used on the bridge of the Star Ship Enterprise. Alternatively the system may initiate a conversation (Alert to Listening again) based on sensor information (for example, in our case the house keys being taken off the hook) an incoming message, or a diary event.

The SALT(E) interaction manager relates to the dialog manager in that the interaction manager handles the timing and determines when to say things while it is left to the dialog manager to decide what to say. The interface can again be described with a class diagram in which a DialogManager extends the InteractionManager implementing the following abstract methods:

```
heardThis(wrdEvent)
getWhatToSay():String
nextEncouragement():String
```

It is of course trivial to implement an Eliza style conversation based on heardThis/getWhatToSay with nextEncouragement taking the role of "nothing matched" patterns. In the case of SERA, the dialog manager is a conventional state based system with states clustered into topics.

The interaction manager also provides two other methods:

```
wakeup()
systemInit(WrdEvent1,wrdEvent2)
```

The first moves the system from Sleeping to Alert and initiates the pause 4 timer. The method systemInit(...) calls heardThis() immediately with wrdEvent1 - note the interaction manager still needs to call getWhatToSay() before anything is said. The second argument is past to heardThis() the next time the system becomes Alert. That is, the next time the user appears and the system moves from Sleeping to Alert, or the next time the system moves from Engaged to Alert. wrdEvent1 is an urgent message - in our case the message that the video recording is on - and wrdEvent2 represents something that can join the queue.

4 How language works (version 3)

The above has been rather low level but hopefully sufficiently brief, while detailed enough to be reproducible. But why is this of interest? Surely this is simply a technical issue that can be left to the RAs - a classic case of "flush pop-rivets" (Vincenti, 1990) which might be critical but is surely, well, boring. This section provides the theoretical background to the claim that managing engagement is critical.

The classic computer science view of human language is that it is some form of debased perfect language (Eco, 1995). In the middle ages perfection was defined in terms of God but to the Modern mind perfection has tended to mean something elegant, concise and unambiguous, typified by predicate calculus. Attempts to make computers understand language have forced the realisation that human languages are primarily driven by convention, highly context sensitive, and rely on the human capability for simile and metaphor. My latest view is that it is worse than that and that we pretty much make it up as we go along. This section briefly introduces a model of language from the Applied Linguistics community and shows how that model makes managing engagement critical.

In 2004 a group of us became interested in the way people tend to swear at conversational agents (de Angeli, 2005). In some work on an animal version of the Turing Test, there is some rather dramatic footage of a dog attacking an AIBO (Kubinyi et al., 2003). The interesting thing is that the dog warns the AIBO (twice) before throwing it across the room. The observation is that dogs, like people, are social animals and that the warning appears to be one mechanism for socialization of the young. When people abuse chat-bots, are they trying to socialize the machine? This of course would not be a concious process but rather normative (Wallis, 2005). This prompted a search for some high level social norm that might explain why people swear at computers. The result of that search was such a rule from the literature on Conversation Analysis or CA.

Paul Seedhouse (Seedhouse, 2004) summarises the outcome of the last 50 years of CA research as with the observation that a conversational partner's utterance will, in the normal case, go **seen but unnoticed**. That is, the utterance is an answer to a question, a response to a greeting or, more formally the second pair part of an adjacency pair. This is something computers can handle. A common occurrence is however where an utterance goes **noticed and accounted for**. In this case the conversational partner does not produce the expected response but what they do say makes sense. Indeed the conversational partner will work hard to produce the accounting. This is Eggins and Slade (Eggins and Slade, 1997) introducing sequential relevance:

> Consider, for example, the two turns at talk below:
>
> A What's that floating in the wine?
>
> B There aren't any other solutions.
>
> You will try very hard to find a way of interpreting B's turn as somehow an answer to A's question, even though there is no obvious link between them, apart from their appearance in sequence. Perhaps you will have decided that B took a common solution to a resistant wine cork and poked it through into the bottle, and it was floating in the wine. Whatever explanation you came up with, it is unlikely that you looked at the example and simply said "it doesn't make sense", so strong is the implication that adjacent turns relate to each other.

Having a machine account for human utterances is of course tricky but conversely the human conversational partner will work hard to account for what are actually machine failings.

If you fail to account for your CP's utterance, then your CP **risks sanction**. When your CP is a chat-bot, that sanction is likely, it seems, to take the form of swearing. As a classic example of a machine's interaction eliciting sanctions, here is a conversation from the 1996 Lobner Competition:

SYSTEM	G'day mate.
JUDGE	G'day. How's it going?
SYSTEM	My mother once said "How it is going is a mystery." She was a bit nuts.
JUDGE	Uh-huh
SYSTEM	Are you still learning to speak, my friend?
JUDGE	NO, no. But your anecdote took me a bit by surprise.
JUDGE	How was your morning?
SYSTEM	Oh well, that's a pity!
JUDGE	I'm sorry; what's a pity?
SYSTEM	Apologies accepted.
JUDGE	I feel compelled to insult you and we've only been talking a minute.
SYSTEM	We are bloody well talking, aren't we?
JUDGE	Oh baby. We sure are. So here are some keywords for you: shit mother baseball.
	...

This was the winning entry from that year but the point is not the system, but how the *human* responds.

There are of course more recent and better funded projects and in particular the DARPA Communicator Programme. The observation is that those systems did well when the human stuck to answering the system's questions and the ASR worked - the seen but unnoticed. When the grounded knowledge was not as the script designers expected however, the system did not have the world knowledge to understand the user's repair strategy. The systems also failed to hand over control to the user (Wallis, 2008). The result was sanction and although swearing is rare – surprising when one listens to the conversations – users did "not want to use the system on a regular basis" (Walker, 2002)

The mechanism for accounting for can be both tactical and strategic. Eliza and Parry were very successful in that user satisfaction was high compared to modern day systems. The mechanism was strategic in those systems in that they provide an accounting for their behaviour – in the first case because the role of psychologist accounts for the endless stream of personal questions, and in the second because being paranoid accounts for the system's odd responses and interests.

4.1 So, engagement?

Why are we interested in engagement? Because in order for the human to "work very hard to find a way of interpreting [what the machine said]" the human must be committed to the conversation. This commitment needs management, and it is the role of the InteractionManager to do this. This is not an issue for a chat bot on a website nor for a system set up for experiments in a laboratory, but becomes a significant issue for an interactive artifact that is permanently in someone's kitchen.

5 Conclusions

Our aim is to study long term relationships between people and robot companions and the intention is to put Nabaztags in an older person's home and see what happens. This is not as straightforward as it may first appear as much of our understanding of these systems is based on demonstrators and experimental trials in which attention is, by the very nature of the trial, directed to the artifact. We introduce the SALT(E) model which separates the dialog manager in to a module that determines *what* to say, and another that determines *when* to say it.

6 Acknowledgments

The research leading to these results has received funding from the European Community's Seventh Framework Programme [FP7/2007-2013] under grant agreement no. 231868. It has also received help from Loquendo that has generously provided the text-to-speech system for our robots.

References

2010. Aged Concern. http://www.ageconcern.org.uk.

Antonella de Angeli. 2005. Stupid computer! abuse and social identity. In Antonella De Angeli, Sheryl Brahnam, and Peter Wallis, editors, *Abuse: the darker side of Human-Computer Interaction (INTERACT '05)*, Rome, September. http://www.agentabuse.org/.

Umberto Eco. 1995. *The Search for the Perfect Language (The Making of Europe)*. Blackwell Publishers, Oxford, UK.

Suzanne Eggins and Diana Slade. 1997. *Analysing Casual Conversation*. Cassell, Wellington House, 125 Strand, London.

2010. Help the Aged. http://www.helptheaged.org.uk.

Jim Hieronymus. 2009. personal communication.

Enikö Kubinyi, Ádám Miklósi, Frédéric Kaplan, Márta Gácsi, ózsef Topál, and Vilmos Csányi. 2003. Social behaviour of dogs encountering AIBO, an animal-like robot in a neutral and in a feeding situation. *Behavioural Proceses*, 65:231–239.

Oli Mival, S. Cringean, and D. Benyon. 2004. Personification technologies: Developing artificial companions for older people. In *CHI Fringe*, Austria.

Darren Moore, John Dines, Mathew Magimai Doss, Jithendra Vepa, Octavian Cheng, and Thomas Hain. 2006. Juicer: A weighted finite state transducer speech decoder. In *MLMI-06*, Washington DC.

Paul Seedhouse. 2004. *The Interactional Architecture of the Language Classroom: A Conversation Analysis Perspective*. Blackwell, September.

Gabriel Skantze. 2007. *Error Handling in Spoken Dialogue Systems - Managing Uncertainty, Grounding and Miscommunication*. Ph.D. thesis, Department of Speech, Music and Hearing, KTH.

Walter G. Vincenti. 1990. *What Engineers know and how they know it: analytical studies from aeronautical history*. The John Hopkins Press Ltd, London.

Marilyn et al Walker. 2002. DARPA communicator evaluation: Progress from 2000 to 2001. In *Proceedings of ICSLP 2002*, Denver, USA.

Peter Wallis, Helen Mitchard, Damian O'Dea, and Jyotsna Das. 2001. Dialogue modelling for a conversational agent. In Markus Stumptner, Dan Corbett, and Mike Brooks, editors, *AI2001: Advances in Artificial Intelligence, 14th Australian Joint Conference on Artificial Intelligence*, Adelaide, Australia. Springer (LNAI 2256).

Peter Wallis. 2005. Robust normative systems: What happens when a normative system fails? In Sheryl Brahnam Antonella De Angeli and Peter Wallis, editors, *Abuse: the darker side of human-computer interaction*, Rome, September.

Peter Wallis. 2008. Revisiting the DARPA communicator data using Conversation Analysis. *Interaction Studies*, 9(3), October.

An Embodied Dialogue System with Personality and Emotions

Stasinos Konstantopoulos

NCSR 'Demokritos', Athens, Greece
konstant@iit.demokritos.gr

Abstract

An enduring challenge in human-computer interaction (HCI) research is the creation of natural and intuitive interfaces. Besides the obvious requirement that such interfaces communicate over modalities such as natural language (especially spoken) and gesturing that are more natural for humans, exhibiting affect and adaptivity have also been identified as important factors to the interface's acceptance by the user. In the work presented here, we propose a novel architecture for affective and multimodal dialogue systems that allows explicit control over the personality traits that we want the system to exhibit. More specifically, we approach personality as a means of synthesising different, and possibly conflicting, adaptivity models into an overall model to be used to drive the interaction components of the system. Furthermore, this synthesis is performed in the presence of domain knowledge, so that domain structure and relations influence the results of the calculation.

1 Introduction

An enduring challenge in human-computer interaction (HCI) research is the creation of natural and intuitive interfaces. Besides the obvious requirement that such interfaces communicate over modalities such as *natural language* (especially spoken) and *gesturing* that are more natural for humans, exhibiting *affect* and *adaptivity* have also been identified as important factors to the interface's acceptance by the user.

We perceive HCI systems as ensembles of interaction modules, each controlling a different interaction modality, and able to modulate their operation depending on external (to the modules themselves) parameters. A central cognitive module deliberates about dialogue acts and orchestrates the interaction modules in order to ensure that such dialogue acts are carried out in a coherent way, keeping uttered content and affect consistent within and across interaction modules.

In this paper we describe work towards this end, carried out in the context of the INDIGO project, and implemented in the form of a *personality module* that complements INDIGO's dialogue manager by calculating parameters related to adaptivity and emotion to be used by the interaction modules in the process of concretely realizing the abstract dialogue-action directives issued by the dialogue manager. This calculation involves the planned act, the user adaptivity model, the system's own goals, but also a machine representation of the *personality* that we want the system to exhibit, so that systems with different personality will react differently even when in the same dialogue state and with the same user or user type.

This is motivated by the fact that, although personality is a characteristically human quality, it has been demonstrated that human users attribute a personality to the computer interfaces they use, regardless of whether one has been explicitly encoded in the system's design (Nass et al., 1995). Furthermore, personality complementarity and similarity are important factors for the acceptance of an interface by a user (Moon and Nass, 1996; Nass and Lee, 2000), so that there is no 'optimal' or 'perfect' system personality, but rather the need to tune system personality to best fit its users.

In the rest of this paper, we will briefly discuss literature on both adaptivity and personality modelling (Section 2), proceed to present the interaction between multimodal dialogue strategies and our personality model (Section 3), and finally conclude (Section 4).

Proceedings of the 2010 Workshop on Companionable Dialogue Systems, ACL 2010, pages 31–36,
Uppsala, Sweden, 15 July 2010.

2 Background

INDIGO in general and our work in particular is, to a large extend, based on work on adaptive natural-language interfaces to databases. The domains of application of these systems have varied from generating personalized encyclopedia entries and museum exhibit descriptions, to supporting the authoring of technical manuals and on-line store catalogues.

2.1 Adaptive HCI

The ILEX system was a major milestone in adaptive *natural language generation* (NLG), emphasising the separation between domain and linguistic resources permitting the *portability* of linguistic resources between domains. ILEX also introduced the notion of a *system agenda* that represents the system's own communicative goals, a significant step in the direction of representing system personality. These system preferences were combined with user preferences and a dynamic *assimilation score* (calculated from interaction history) to estimate a single preference factor for the various facts in the database for the purposes of selecting the content that is to be included in the description of each object (Ó Donnell et al., 2001).

ILEX, however, offered no theory about where interest and importance come from or how to combine them; arbitrary values had to be provided for all objects in the database and the combined preference was derived by multiplying the three factors (importance, interest, and assimilation) regardless of how each object is related to other interesting or important objects in the collection or what other relevant and semantically similar objects have been assimilated.

Building upon ILEX, the M-PIRO system extended user model preferences to influence surface realization besides content selection, so that different surface forms would be generated to realize the same abstract piece of information for different users (Isard et al., 2003). This was achieved by explicitly representing the grammar fragments that could be used to realize different types of facts (properties of the object being described) and then extending the user interests mechanism to also select which grammar fragment is more 'interesting' (or, rather, appropriate) to realize a particular piece of information for a particular user model.

By comparison to ILEX, M-PIRO offered greater flexibility and linguistic variation, as well as language portability by allowing the combination of different grammars with the same domain or user models. On the other hand, the, even rudimentary, ability to combine user and system preferences was dropped and user model authoring became practically unmanageable due the size and complexity of user models.

With the emergence of the Semantic Web, it became obvious that representation technologies such as RDF and OWL offered an opportunity to reduce the authoring effort by operating upon pre-existing OWL ontologies. This motivated the development of the NATURALOWL/ELEON system. NATURALOWL is a template-based NLG engine, explicitly designed for generating natural language descriptions of ontological entities, based on such entities' abstract properties (Galanis and Androutsopoulos, 2007). The ELEON authoring tool (Konstantopoulos et al., 2009) can be used to annotate OWL ontologies with linguistic and content-selection resources and inter-operates with NATURALOWL which can use such annotations to generate descriptions of ontological objects.

2.2 Emotions and personality

Another relevant line of research is centred around *affective interaction* and *intelligent virtual agents*. The main focus here is the modelling and mimicking of the various affective markers that people use when they communicate, aiming at more natural and seamless human-computer interaction.

Such affective systems are modulated by *personality representations* varying from fully-blown cognitive architectures (Vankov et al., 2008) to relatively simpler personality models. The *OCEAN* or *Big Five* model, in particular, a standard framework in psychology (Norman, 1963; Costa and McCrae, 1992), is used to represent personality in a variety of virtual agents and avatars capable for multi-modal communication acts such as speech and facial expressions (Strauss and Kipp, 2008; Kasap et al., 2009). Such systems are typically rich in visual expression, but lack sophistication in natural language generation, knowledge representation and dialogue structure.

The PERSONAGE and INDIGO systems, on the other hand, move in the area between these systems and the database-access systems discussed above: PERSONAGE develops a comprehensive

Figure 1: An INDIGO robot interacting with *Hellenic Cosmos* personnel during preliminary trials, September 2009.

theory of using OCEAN parameters to control natural language interaction from lexical choice to syntax, pragmatics, and planning, but is restricted to text generation and no other communication modalities are covered (Mairesse and Walker, 2007). The INDIGO dialogue system emphasises multi-modality as it is embodied in a robot capable of multi-modal interaction. INDIGO uses OCEAN to combine a separate user model and system profile into a single parameter set used to parametrize a number of interaction components, such as a virtual avatar capable of displaying emotions, the NLG engine, the text-to-speech engine, the dialogue manager, etc.

3 A dialogue system with personality

The INDIGO system has been fielded at the *Hellenic Cosmos* cultural centre,[1] where it provides personalized tours with historical, architectural, and cultural information about the buildings of the Ancient Agora of Athens (Figure 1).

The *dialogue manager* (DM, Matheson et al., 2009), implemented using TrindiKit,[2] assumes the *information-state and update* approach to dialogue management (Traum and Larsson, 2003). The information state stores information such as dialogue history and current robot position. Input from the sensors (ASR, vision, laser tracker, and touchscreen) is processed by update rules which heuristically fuse multimodal (and possibly contradicting) sensory input and implement generic (i.e., domain and personality-independent) dialogue strategies. These strategies deliberate about the next action that the robot will take, such as moving to a different section of the exhibition, offering a menu of choices, or describing an item.

One notable strategy implemented in the DM is the *Move On Related* strategy (Bohus and Rudnicky, 2008), the system's fallback when user input cannot be confidently recognized even after fusing all input modalities. In such situations, DM uses the combined preference factors to choose the most preferred exhibit within the ontological class that is the current focus of the discourse. If there is an instance in this class with a clear preference, DM assumes this as the user response; if, on the other hand, there is no instance with significantly higher preference than the rest, DM prompts the user to repeat their answer or use the touchscreen.

The other notable, and widely used, strategy is the one that drives the two loops shown in Figure 2, in response to a user request for content: one pertaining to dynamically realizing a personalized description of an object of the domain ontology and one pertaining to updating the system's emotion and mood.

3.1 Content selection and realization loop

Once the DM has resolved that the next robot action will be the description of a domain ontology object, the personality-driven preferences are used to select which properties of this object will be included in the description. These preferences are calculated taking into account a combined user-system preference (Konstantopoulos et al., 2008) as well as a dynamic *assimilation score*, calculated from interaction history, which balances between the gratuitous and tiring repetition of high-preference material and simply rotating through the list of properties of an object.

The chosen content is then used by the NATURALOWL NLG engine (Galanis and Androutsopoulos, 2007) to plan and realize a personalized textual description of the object. Besides selecting what to include in a description, preference is used by NATURALOWL to annotate the generated text with directives, such as *emphasis*, for the text-to-speech effector that drives the robot's speakers.

The combined user-system preference stems from associating domain objects with content-selection parameters, using an representation developed for NATURALOWL and extended in INDIGO to provide for representing not only user models but also *system profiles* that establish the system's own goals and preferences (Konstan-

[1]See also http://www.hellenic-cosmos.gr

[2]See http://sourceforge.net/projects/trindikit/

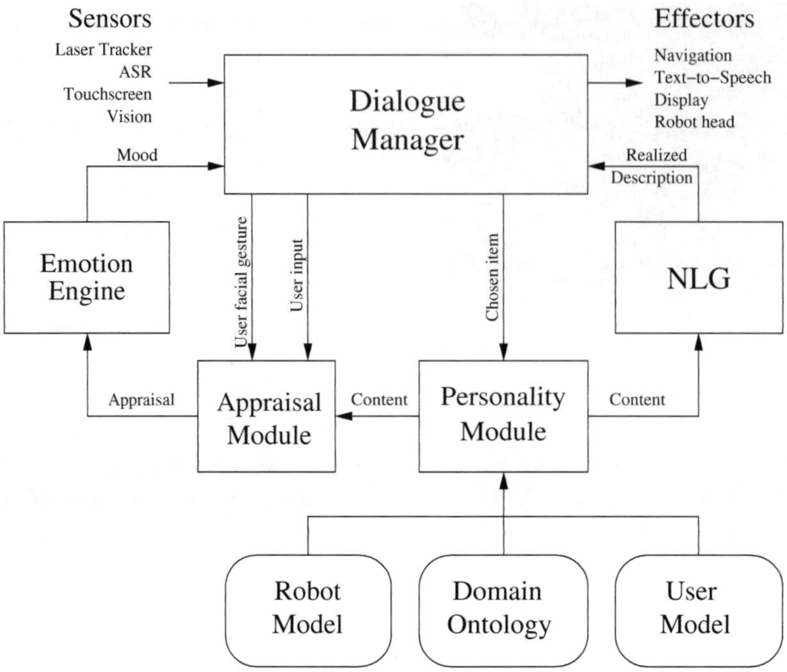

Figure 2: Overall architecture of the dialogue system.

topoulos et al., 2009).

Emotional and, in general, behavioural variation among different instantiations of the system is achieved through *synthetic personality models* that assert different points of balance between the (potentially) conflicting user and system preferences. What is of particular importance is that the the combined user-system preference is not estimated in isolation for each and every ontological object as was the case in ILEX, but by axiomatizing how preference is 'transferred' between domain objects based on their semantic relations. This is achieved by defining personality in terms of logic clauses that link the preferences of an object not only to its user and system preferences, but also to those of objects it semantically relates with.

3.2 Emotional appraisal and update loop

The system emotionally appraises user actions as well as its own actions. With respect to its own actions, the preference factors for the properties selected to describe an object reflect the robot's being excited or bored to discuss the current subject.

Appraisal of user actions stems from vision and speech analysis to reflect the impact of the *manner* of what the user said. More specifically, facial gesture recognition is used to detect emotional signs (such as smiling) besides detecting affirmative and negative nods and similar signs that are fused with the results of speech recognition.

As user utterances are mostly short and incomplete answers to questions such as 'Would you like to hear more about this monument?' or 'Which monument would you like me to talk about?' we cannot detect emotion based on linguistic meaning or syntactic structure, but rather concentrate on extracting useful prosodic and linguistic features such the length of the last syllable in an utterance or whether the first word of the utterance is an *wh*-word.[3] Although these features are not by themselves indicative of emotion, they are indicative of prosody and their combination with segmental features (referring to the acoustic form) extracted directly from the speech signal was shown to improve emotion estimation.

Emotional appraisal is used by an *emotion simulator* (Kasap et al., 2009) that uses the system's personality traits (OCEAN vector) to model how dialogue acts affect the system's emotional state. This emotion simulator updates the system's internal short-term *emotional state* and long-term *mood* by applying an update function on the current state and the *emotional appraisal* of each dialogue act. The OCEAN parameters act as parameters of the update function, so that, for example,

[3]Where, what, who, etc.

neuroticism (i.e., 'tendency to distress') makes the update function tend towards negative emotions, whereas agreeableness (i.e., 'sympathetic') makes it more directly reflect the user's emotions.

The speech synthesiser and the robot's animatronic head reflect emotional state as voice modulations and facial expressions, whereas mood is taken into account by the DM when deliberating about the robot's next dialogue action.

4 Conclusions

In this paper we have approached personality as a means of synthesising different, and possibly conflicting, adaptivity models into an overall model to be used to drive the interaction components of the system. Furthermore, this synthesis is performed in the presence of domain knowledge, so that domain structure and relations influence the results of the calculation.

We thusly explore the *self vs. other* aspect of personality modelling, theoretically interesting but also practically important as we cleanly separate adaptivity and profiling data that refers the system from that which refers to the user. This follows up on the tradition of the line of systems stemming from ILEX, where increasingly separable models (domain vs. NLG resources, the latter later broken down between linguistic and adaptivity resources) have allowed for such hard-to-create resources to be re-used.

Acknowledgements

The work described in this paper was funded by the FP6-IST project INDIGO, that developed and advanced human-robot interaction technology, enabling robots to perceive natural human behaviour and act in ways that are more familiar to humans. To achieve its goals, INDIGO advanced various technologies, which it integrated in a robotic platform.

More details are availble from the project website, `http://www.ics.forth.gr/indigo`

References

Dan Bohus and Alex Rudnicky. 2008. Sorry, I didn't catch that. In Laila Dybkjær and Wolfgang Minker, editors, *Recent Trends in Discourse and Dialogue*, volume 39 of *Text, Speech and Language Technology*, chapter 6, pages 123–154. Springer Netherlands.

P. T. Costa and R. R. McCrae. 1992. Normal personality assessment in clinical practice: The NEO personality inventory. *Psychological Assessment*, 4(5–13).

Dimitris Galanis and Ion Androutsopoulos. 2007. Generating multilingual descriptions from linguistically annotated OWL ontologies: the NaturalOWL system. In *Proceedings of the 11th European Workshop on Natural Language Generation (ENLG 2007), Schloss Dagstuhl, Germany*, pages 143–146.

Amy Isard, Jon Oberlander, Ion Androutsopoulos, and Colin Matheson. 2003. Speaking the users' languages. *IEEE Intelligent Systems*, 18(1):40–45.

Zerrin Kasap, Maher Ben Moussa, Parag Chaudhuri, and Nadia Magnenat-Thalmann. 2009. Making them remember: Emotional virtual characters with memory. In Tiffany Barnes, L. Miguel Encarnção, and Chris Shaw, editors, *Serious Games, Special Issue of IEEE Computer Graphics and Applications*. IEEE.

Stasinos Konstantopoulos, Vangelis Karkaletsis, and Dimitris Bilidas. 2009. An intelligent authoring environment for abstract semantic representations of cultural object descriptions. In Lars Borin and Piroska Lendvai, editors, *Proceedings of EACL-09 Workshop on Language Technology and Resources for Cultural Heritage, Social Sciences, Humanities, and Education* (LaTeCH-SHELT&R 2009), Athens, 30 Mar 2009, pages 10–17.

Stasinos Konstantopoulos, Vangelis Karkaletsis, and Colin Matheson. 2008. Robot personality: Representation and externalization. In *Proceedings of ECAI-08 Workshop on Computational Aspects of Affective and Emotional Interaction (CAFFEi 2008), Patras, Greece, July 21st, 2008*, pages 5–13.

François Mairesse and Marilyn Walker. 2007. PERSONAGE: Personality generation for dialogue. In *Proceedings of the 45th Annual Meeting of the Association for Computational Linguistics (ACL)*. Prague.

Colin Matheson, Amy Isard, Jon Oberlander, Stasinos Konstantopoulos, and Vangelis Karkaletsis. 2009. Multimodal human-robot dialogue management. INDIGO Deliverable 4.1 (public).

Youngme Moon and Clifford Nass. 1996. Adaptive agents and personality change: complementarity versus similarity as forms of adaptation. In *Proceedings SIGCHI Conference on Human Factors in Computing Systems*, Vancouver, BC, Canada, 1996. SIG on Computer-Human Interaction, ACM, New York, U.S.A.

Clifford Nass and Kwan Min Lee. 2000. Does computer-generated speech manifest personality? an experimental test of similarity-attraction. In *Proceedings SIGCHI Conference on Human factors in Computing Systems*, The Hague, 2000. SIG on Computer-Human Interaction, ACM, New York, U.S.A.

Clifford Nass, Youngme Moon, B. Fogg, and B. Reeves. 1995. Can computer personalities be human personalities? *International Journal of Human-Computer Studies*, 43:223–239.

W. T. Norman. 1963. Toward an adequate taxonomy of personality attributes: Replicated factor structure in peer nomination personality rating. *Journal of Abnormal and Social Psychology*, 66:574–583.

Michael Ó Donnell, Chris Mellish, Jon Oberlander, and A. Knott. 2001. ILEX: an architecture for a dynamic hypertext generation system. *Natural Language Engineering*, 7(3):225–250.

Martin Strauss and Michael Kipp. 2008. ERIC: a generic rule-based framework for an affective embodied commentary agent. In *Proceedings of the 7th international joint conference on Autonomous agents and multiagent systems (AAMAS 08), Estoril, Portugal, 2008*, pages 97–104.

David Traum and Steffan Larsson. 2003. The information state approach to dialogue management. In Jan van Kuppevelt and Ronnie Smith, editors, *Current and New Directions in Discourse and Dialogue*. Kluwer Academic Publishers, Dordrecht, the Netherlands.

Ivan Vankov, Kiril Kiryazov, and Maurice Grinberg. 2008. Introducing emotions in an analogy-making model. In *Proceedings of 30th Annual Meeting of the Cognitive Science Society (CogSci 2008), Washington D.C.*

'How was your day?'

S. G. Pulman, J. Boye
University of Oxford
sgp@clg.ox.ac.uk

M. Cavazza, C. Smith
Teesside University
m.o.cavazza@tees.ac.uk

R. S. de la Cámara
Telefonica I+D
e.rsai@tid.es

Abstract

We describe a 'How was your day?' (HWYD) Companion whose purpose is to establish a comforting and supportive relationship with a user via a conversation on a variety of work-related topics. The system has several fairly novel features aimed at increasing the naturalness of the interaction: a rapid 'short loop' response primed by the results of acoustic emotion analysis, and an 'interruption manager', enabling the user to interrupt lengthy or apparently inappropriate system responses, prompting a replanning of behaviour on the part of the system. The 'long loop' also takes into account the emotional state of the user, but using more conventional dialogue management and planning techniques. We describe the architecture and components of the implemented prototype HWYD system.

1 Introduction

As the existence of this workshop shows, there is a good deal of interest in a type of spoken language dialogue system distinct from the traditional task-based models used for booking airline tickets and the like. The purpose of these 'social agent' systems is to be found in the relationship they can establish with human users, rather than on the assistance the agent can provide in giving information or solving a problem. Designing such agents provides many significant technical challenges, requiring progress in the integration of linguistic communication and non-verbal behaviour for affective dialogue (André et al. 2004). In this paper, we present the implementation of a Companion Embodied Conversational Agent (ECA) which integrates emotion and sentiment detection with more traditional dialogue components.

2 From Dialogue to Conversation

Most spoken language dialogue systems are 'task-based': they aim at getting from the user values for a fixed number of slots in some template. When enough values have been found, the filled template is sent off to some back-end system so that the task in question - ordering a pizza, booking a ticket etc. - can be carried out. However, a social Companion agent assumes a kind of conversation not necessarily connected to any immediate task, and which may not follow the conventions associated with task-driven dialogues, for example, the relatively strict turn-taking of task-based dialogue. In everyday life, many interhuman conversations see one of the participants producing lengthy descriptions of events, without this corresponding to any specific request or overall conversational purpose. Our objective was to support such free conversation, whilst still obtaining meaningful answers from the agent, in the form of advice appropriate both to the affective and informational content of the conversation. In order to balance the constraints of free conversation with those of tractability, we have deliberately opted for a single-domain conversation, in contrast with both small talk (Bickmore and Cassell, 1999) and 'chatterbot' approaches. Our HWYD domain involves typical events and topics of conversation in the workplace, ranging from the relatively mundane - meeting colleagues, getting delayed by traffic, project deadlines - to rather more important - promotions, firings, arguments, office politics - designed to evoke stronger emotions and hence more affective dialogues.

However, our HWYD Companions retains some features of a typical task based system, in that each of these subtopics can be thought of as a task or information extraction template. Unfilled slots will drive the dialogue manager to question the user for possible values. When enough slots

Proceedings of the 2010 Workshop on Companionable Dialogue Systems, ACL 2010, pages 37–42,
Uppsala, Sweden, 15 July 2010. ©2010 Association for Computational Linguistics

are filled, the initiative will be passed to an 'affective strategy' module, which will generate a longer response designed to empathise appropriately with the user over that particular topic.

3 System Overview and Architecture

The HWYD Companion integrates 15 different software components, covering at least to some degree all the necessary aspects of multimodal affective input and output: including speech recognition (ASR, using Dragon Naturally Speaking), emotional speech recognition (AA: the EmoVoice system (Vogt et al. 2008)), turn detection (ATT), Dialogue Act segmentation and tagging (DAT), Emotional modelling (EM), Sentiment Analysis (SA) (Moilanen et al. 2007), Natural Language Understanding (NLU), Dialogue Management (DM), user modelling and a knowledge base (KB/UM), an 'Affective Strategy Module' (ASM) generating complex system replies, Natural Language Generation (NLG), Speech Synthesis (TTS), an avatar (ECA), and Multimodal control of the ECA persona (MFM): gesture and facial expression, supported by the Haptek animation toolkit. Clearly the use of Naturally Speaking imposes on us speaker dependence, since the system needs training: in the scenario we have chosen this is in fact not too unrealistic an assumption, but this is merely a practical decision - we are not doing research on speech recognition as such in this project and so want to get as good a recognition rate as possible.

The software architecture of the prototype relies on the Inamode Framework developed by Telefnica I+D. Communication between modules follows a blackboard-like paradigm, in which central hubs broadcast any incoming message from any module to all of the other modules that are connected to it. Figure 1 below shows the system architecture, and Figure 2 shows one version of what is on the screen when the system is running.

4 Emotional Feedback Loops

Recognising and responding appropriately to different emotions is an important aspect of a social agent. In our HWYD Companion, emotion and sentiment are used in two ways: firstly, to provide immediate feedback to a user utterance (given that there will inevitably be some delay in the response from natural language and dialogue processing modules) and secondly to inform the more extended responses given by the system when it has learned enough about the current sub-topic. There are two feedback loops: the 'short loop' (response time < 700 ms) provides an immediate backchannel, and its main purpose is to maintain contact and keep the communication alive and realistic. This is achieved by matching the nonverbal response (gesture, facial expression) of the avatar to the emotional speech parameters detected by EmoVoice prior to affective fusion (where the emotion detected from speech and the sentiment value detected from the corresponding text are merged: see below), and occasionally including an appropriate verbal acknowledgement, on a random basis to avoid acknowledging all user utterances. The short loop essentially aligns the ECA response to the user's attitude, thus showing empathy. (We should also use SA for this, but currently processing speed is not fast enough).

The 'major loop' (response time < 3000 ms) involves the ECA's full response to the user utterance in terms of both verbal and non-verbal behaviour. There are effectively two sources of system output: the dialogue manager engages with the user to find out what happened during their work day, and will ask questions, or drop into clarificatory sub-dialogues, gradually building up a complex event description along with an assessment of the prevailing emotions of the speaker. When sufficient information has been gathered, control is passed to an 'affective strategy module' which will produce a longer output, typically advice or warning in response to the user's recollection of his daily events.

The system also includes an interruption manager which detects interruption and barge-in by the user, resulting in the immediate suspension of the current system utterance, triggering the processing of any content specific to the interrupting utterance, and consequent replanning on the part of other modules to produce an appropriate response. Such an interruption is illustrated in Figure 1. The design of such an interruption manager in a system with so many separate modules is quite challenging, in fact: the system is described further in Crook et al. (2010).

The ECA listens sympathetically to the user's account of work difficulties, whilst also reacting to apparent discrepancies between perceived mood and the affective content of the recognised events. In the following example from a real conversation,

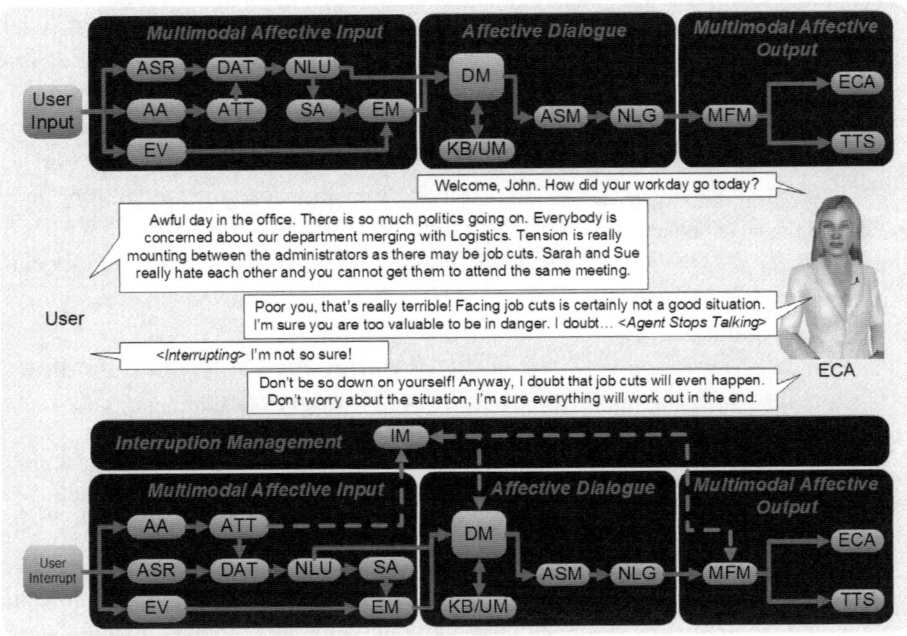

Figure 1: Overview of the System Architecture illustrating the information flow between modules.

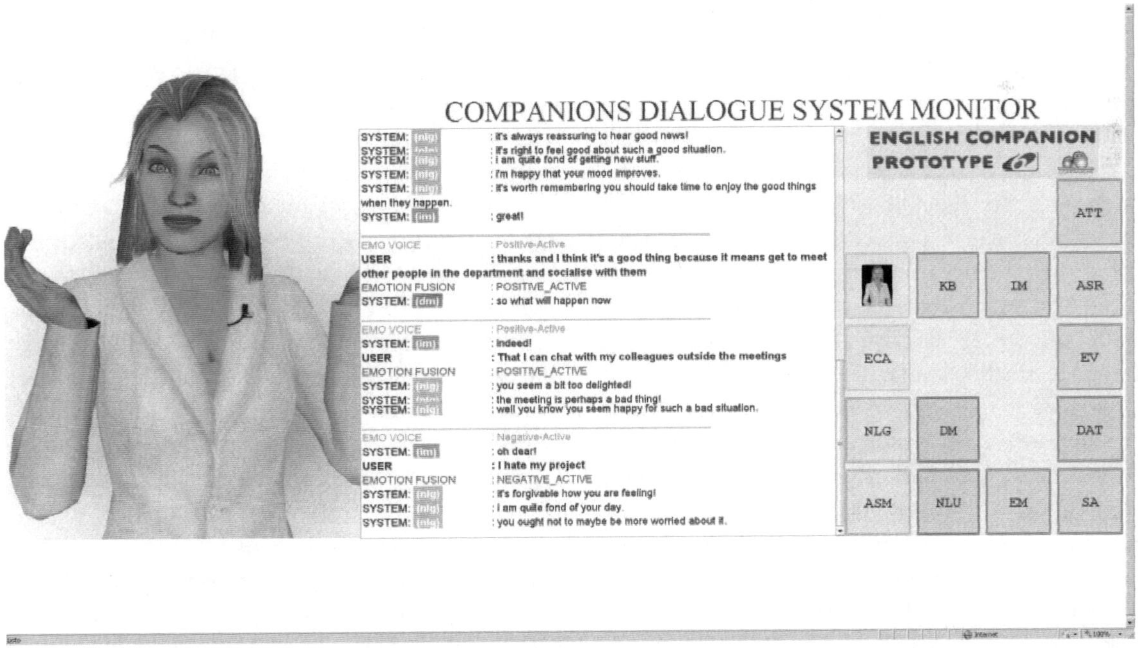

Figure 2: The HWYD Companion in operation: the central portion of the screen traces the dialogue, whilst the right-hand one displays which current software module is activated.

the user announces a company restructuring, but in a rather cheerful tone. Notice that some of the English is a little strange: the generator produces a mixture of genuinely generated output along with some canned text.

User: I have just learnt that my department is going to be merged with the Barcelona one (EMOTION FUSION: POSITIVE_ACTIVE)
System: You seem a bit too ecstatic! I'm doubtful that your workload could be maintained.

Every time the Companion has gathered sufficient information it will try to respond more globally to the situation at hand. In the following example (see also Figure 2), after the user has expressed different sorts of concerns, the Companion picks on the latest (positive) information to summarise the few positive elements it picked from the conversation:

User: yes but one good thing anyway we had a new coffee machine arrived today (EMOTION FUSION: POSITIVE_ACTIVE)
System: it's always reassuring to hear good news! It's right to feel good about such a good situation. I am quite fond of getting new stuff. I'm happy that your mood improves. It's worth remembering you should take time to enjoy the good things when they happen.

5 Emotional Modelling and Fusion

Two different modules analyse the emotional content of user utterances: an emotional speech recognition system (EmoVoice (Vogt et al. 2008) which returns information indicating both the arousal and valence of the acoustic properties of the user's speech as negative passive, negative-active, neutral, positive-active or positive-passive, and a text-based Sentiment Analysis module which operates on the utterance transcript after its recognition by the ASR module. The SA module operates in a compositional way and is able to classify linguistic units of any syntactic type: noun phrases, clauses, sentences etc. It is also able to assign a 'strength' of the sentiment expressed. In the current implementation it simply classifies clauses as either negative, neutral or positive. These two emotional inputs are then merged by a fusion procedure, whose purpose is to provide an aggregate emotional category to be attached to the event description template produced by the NLU and DM module. Essentially, the mechanism for affective fusion consists in overriding the valence category of EmoVoice with the one obtained by SA every time the confidence score attached to EmoVoice is below a preset value (depending on the competing valence categories). Fusion is currently an underdeveloped module: for example, detecting mismatches between speech and language emotion and sentiment values could lead to the recognition of irony, sarcasm etc. (Tepperman et al. 2006). Saying an intrinsically negative thing in a positive and cheerful way, or the other way round, suggests that the speaker is trying for some special effect.

6 Natural Language Understanding and Dialogue Management

The task of the NLU module is to recognise a specific set of events reported by the user within utterances which can be of significant length ($>$ 50 words) and which can be difficult to parse due to speech recognition errors. This led us to follow an Information Extraction (IE) approach to dialogue analysis (see Jönsson et al. 2004), using shallow syntactic and semantic processing to find instantiations of event templates. The NLU component of the HWYD Companion demonstration system takes the 1-best output from the speech recogniser (currently: work in progress will take n-best), which has already been segmented into dialogue-act sized utterances (by the DAT module which simultaneously segments and labels the recogniser output: see Figure 1). So, for example, a sequence like 'It was okay there are not many projects at the moment so it is very quiet would be segmented into three separate dialogue acts. The utterances are then part-of-speech tagged and chunked into Noun Phrase (NP) and Verb Group (VG) units. VGs consist of a main verb and any auxiliary verbs or semantically important adverbs. Both of these stages are carried out by a Hidden Markov Model trained on the Penn Treebank, although some customisation has been carried out for this application: relevant vocabulary added and some probabilities re-estimated to reflect properties of the application. NP and VG chunks are then classified into 'Named Entity' classes, some of which are the usual *person*, *organisation*, *time* etc. but others of which are specific to the scenario, as is traditional in IE: e.g. salient work events, expressions of emotion, organisational structure etc. Named Entity classification, in the absence of domain specific training data, is carried out via hand-written pattern matching rules and gazetteers. Each chunk is further annotated with features encoding the head word, stem form, polarity, agreement features, relevant modifiers, etc. for later syntactic and semantic processing. The NPs and VGs are represented as unification grammar categories containing information about the internal structure of the constituents.

The next stage applies unification based syntax rules which combine NP and VG chunks into larger constituents. These rules are of two types: most are syntactically motivated and are attempting to build a parse tree from which main grammatical relations (subject, object, etc.) can be recognised. These have coverage of the main syntactic constructs of English. But within the same formalism we add domain specific Information Extraction type patterns, looking out for particular constellations of entities and events relevant to the HWYD scenario, for example 'argument at work between X and Y', or 'meeting with X about Y'. Processing is non-deterministic and so sentences will get many analyses. We use a 'shortest path through the chart heuristic to select an interpretation. This is far from perfect, and we are currently working on a separate more motivated disambiguation module.

The final stage of processing before the Dialogue Manager takes over is to perform reference resolution for pronouns and definite NPs. This module is based partly on the system described by Kennedy and Boguraev 1996, with the various weighting factors based on theirs, but designed so that the weights can be trained given appropriate data. Currently we are collecting such data and the present set of weights are taken from Kennedy and Boguraev but with additional salience given to the domain-specific named entity classes. Each referring NP gives rise to a discourse referent, and these are grouped into coreference classes based on grammatical, semantic, and salience properties.

The DM maintains an information state containing all objects mentioned during the conversation, and uses this information to decide whether the objects referred to in the utterance are salient or not. The DM also uses type information to interpret elliptical answers to questions (System: 'Who was at the meeting?' User: 'Nigel.'). After the user's utterance has been interpreted in its dialogue context and the information state has been updated, the dialogue manager decides on the appropriate response. If a new object has been introduced by the user, the DM adds a goal to its agenda to talk about that object. For instance, if a new person is mentioned, the DM will ask questions about the user's relation to that person, etc.

For each turn of the dialogue, the DM chooses which topic to pursue next by considering all the currently un-satisfied goals on the agenda and heuristically rating them for importance. The heuristics employed use factors such as recency in the dialogue history, general importance, and emotional value associated with the goal. We are currently exploring the use of reinforcement learning with a reward function based on the results of SA on the users input to choose goals in a more natural way. The DM also has the option of invoking the ASM (described below) to generate an appropriate answer, in the cases where the user says something highly emotive. Again, this is a decision that could involve reinforcement learning, and we are exploring this in our current work.

The joint operation of the NLU and the DM hence supports a kind of IE or task-specific template-filling: the content of the user's utterances, prompted by questions from the DM, provides the information necessary to fill a template to the point where the ASM can take over. The number of templates for domain events is significantly higher than in traditional IE or task-based dialogue systems, however, since the HWYD Companion currently instantiates more than 30 templates, and will eventually cover around 50.

7 Affective Dialogue Strategies

Once the NLU and DM have a sufficiently instantiated template, which also records emotional value, it is passed to the ASM. This controls the generation of longer ECA narrative replies which aim at influencing the user by providing advice or reassurance. Our overall framework for influence is inspired by the work of Bremond 1973. The narrative is constituted by a set of argumentative statements which can be based on emotional operators (e.g. **show-empathy**) or specific communicative operators. The ASM is based on a Hierarchical Task Network (HTN) planner (Nau et al 2004), which works through recursive decomposition of a high level task into sub-tasks until we reach a plan of sub-tasks that can be directly executed. The operators constituting the plan generated by the HTN implement Bremond's theory of influence by emphasising the determinants of the event reported by the user. For instance, various operators can emphasise or play down the event consequences (**emphasise-outcome-importance, emphasise-outcome-justification, emphasise-outcome-warning**) or comment on additional factors that may affect the course of events (**commend-enabler, reassure-helper**). The planner uses a set of 25 operators, each of which can be in addition instantiated to incorporate specific elements of the event. Overall this supports the generation of hundreds of significantly different influencing strategies.

8 Results and Conclusions

We have described an initial, fully-implemented prototype of a Companion ECA supporting free conversation, including affective aspects, over a variety of everyday work-related topics. The system has been demonstrated extensively outside of its development group and was regularly able to sustain consistent dialogues with an average duration exceeding 20 minutes. The Companion ECA recently won the best demonstration prize at AAMAS 2010,the 9th International Conference on Autonomous Agents and Multiagent Systems, Toronto, which is some subjective indication at least that its behaviour is of some interest outside of the project which developed it.

However, we have not yet systematically evaluated the ECA, although this task has begun (Webb et al. 2010). The question of evaluation for systems like this is in fact a rather difficult one, since unlike task-based systems there is no simple measure of success. In our current work we aim to conduct extensive trials with real users and via interview and questionnaires to get some useful measure of how natural and 'companionable' the system is perceived to be.

In other current work we are, as mentioned above, experimenting with reinforcement learning where the reward function is based on the emotion and sentiment detected in the user's input. We are collecting data via Amazon's Mechanical Turk and hope to be able to show how the ECA can develop different 'personalities' depending on how this reward function is defined. For example, we could imagine using simulated dialogues to produce a Companion that was relentlessly cheerful, producing positive outputs whatever the input. Alternatively, we could produce a 'mirror' Companion which simply reflected the mood of the user. We could even produce a 'misery loves company' Companion which, instead of trying to cheer the user up when recognising negative sentiment or emotion, could reply in an equally negative manner.

Acknowledgements

This work was funded by the Companions project (http://www.companions-project.org) sponsored by the European Commission as part of the Information Society Technologies (IST) programme under EC grant number IST-FP6-034434. The EmoVoice system has been used courtesy of the Multimedia Concepts and Applications Group of the University of Augsburg. Other contributors to the prototype described in this paper are Karo Moilanen, and from the COMPANIONS consortium: David Benyon, Jay Bradley, Daniel Charlton, WeiWei Cheng, Morena Danieli, Simon Dobnik, Carlos Sanchez Fernandez, Debora Field, Mari Carmen Rodriguez Gancedo, Jose Relano Gil, Ramon Granell, Jaakko Hakulinen, Preben Hansen, Sue Harding, Topi Hurtig, Oli Mival, Roger Moore, Olov Stahl, Markku Turunen, Enrico Zovato.

References

André, E., Dybkjr, L., Minker, W., and Heisterkamp, P. (Eds.), 2004, *Affective Dialogue Systems* Lecture Notes in Computer Science 3068, Springer.

Bickmore, T., and Cassell, J., 1999. *Small Talk and Conversational Storytelling in Embodied Interface Agents.* Proceedings of the AAAI Fall Symposium on Narrative Intelligence, pp. 87-92. November 5-7, Cape Cod, MA.

Bremond, C., 1973, *Logique du Récit*, Paris: Editions du Seuil.

Cavazza, M., Pizzi, D., Charles, F., Vogt, T. And André, E. 2009, *Emotional input for character-based interactive storytelling.* International Joint Conference on Autonomous Agents and Multi-Agents Systems 2009, pp. 313-320.

Nigel Crook, Cameron Smith, Marc Cavazza, Stephen Pulman, Roger Moore, Johan Boye, 2010, *Handling User Interruptions in an Embodied Conversational Agent* Proceedings of International Workshop on Interacting with ECAs as Virtual Characters, AAMAS 2010.

Jönsson, A., Andén, F., Degerstedt, L., Flycht-Eriksson, A., Merkel, M., and Norberg, S., 2004, *Experiences from combining dialogue system development with information extraction techniques*, in: Mark T. Maybury (Ed), New Directions in Question Answering, AAAI/MIT Press.

Kennedy and B. Boguraev, 1996, *Anaphora for everyone: Pronominal anaphora resolution without a parser.* Proceedings of the 16th International Conference on Computational Linguistics, Copenhagen, ACL, pp 113-118.

Moilanen, K. and Pulman, S. G. , 2007, *Sentiment Composition*, Proceedings of the Recent Advances in Natural Language Processing International Conference (RANLP-2007), pp 378–382.

Nau, D., Ghallab, M., Traverso, P., 2004,*Automated Planning: Theory and Practice*, Morgan Kaufmann Publishers Inc., San Francisco, CA.

J Tepperman, D Traum, and S Narayanan, 2006, *'Yeah right': Sarcasm recognition for spoken dialogue systems*, Interspeech 2006, Pittsburgh, PA, 2006.

Vogt, T., André, E. and Bee, N., 2008 *EmoVoice - A framework for online recognition of emotions from voice.* In: Proceedings of Workshop on Perception and Interactive Technologies for Speech-Based Systems, Springer, Kloster Irsee, Germany, (June 2008).

Webb, N., D. Benyon, P. Hansen and O. Mival, 2010, *Evaluating Human-Machine Conversation for Appropriateness*, in proceedings of the 7th International Conference on Language Resources and Evaluation (LREC2010), Valletta, Malta.

VCA: An Experiment With A Multiparty Virtual Chat Agent

Samira Shaikh[1], Tomek Strzalkowski[1, 2], Sarah Taylor[3], Nick Webb[1]
[1]ILS Institute, University at Albany, State University of New York
[2]Institute of Computer Science, Polish Academy of Sciences
[3]Advancded Technology Office, Lockheed Martin IS&GS
E-mail: ss578726@albany.edu, tomek@albany.edu

Abstract

The purpose of this research was to advance the understanding of the behavior of small groups in online chat rooms. The research was conducted using Internet chat data collected through planned exercises with recruited participants. Analysis of the collected data led to construction of preliminary models of social behavior in online discourse. Some of these models, e.g., how to effectively change the topic of conversation, were subsequently implemented into an automated Virtual Chat Agent (VCA) prototype. VCA has been demonstrated to perform effectively and convincingly in Internet conversation in multiparty chat environments.

1 Introduction

Internet chat rooms provide a ready means of communication for people of most age groups these days. More often than not, these virtual chat rooms have multiple participants conversing on a wide variety of topics, using a highly informal and free-form text dialect. An increasing use of virtual chat rooms by a variety of demographics such as small children and impressionable youth leads to the risk of exploitation by deceitful individuals or organizations. Such risks might be reduced by presence of virtual chat agents that could keep conversations from progressing into certain topics by changing the topic of conversation.

Our aim was to study the behavior of small groups of online chat participants and derive models of social phenomena that occur frequently in a virtual chat environment. We used the MPC chat corpus (Shaikh et al., 2010), which is 20 hours of multi-party chat data collected through a series of carefully designed online chat sessions. Chat data collected from public chat rooms, while easily available, presents significant concerns regarding its adaptability for our research use. Publicly available chat data is completely anonymous, has a high level of noise and lack of focus, in addition to engendering user privacy issues for its use in modeling tasks. The MPC corpus was used in (1) understanding how certain social behaviors are reflected in language and (2) building an automated chat agent that could effectively achieve certain (initially limited) social objectives in the chat-room. A brief description of the MPC corpus and its relevant characteristics is given in Section 3 of this paper.

One specific phenomenon of social behavior we wanted to model was an effective change of conversation topic, when a participant or a group of participants deliberately (if perhaps only temporarily) shift the discussion to a different, possibly related topic. Both success and failure of these actions was of interest because the outcome depended upon the choice of utterance, the persons to whom it was addressed, their reaction, and the time when it was produced. Our analysis of the corpus for such phenomena led to the use of an annotation scheme that allows us to annotate for topic and focus change in conversation. We describe the annotation scheme used in Section 4.

We constructed an autonomous virtual chat agent (VCA) that could achieve initially limited social goals in a chat room with human participants. We used a novel approach of exploiting the topic of conversation underway to search the web and find related topics that could be inserted in the conversation to change its flow. We tested the first prototype with the capability to opportunistically change to topic of conversation using a combination of linguistic, dialogic, and topic reference devices, which we observed effectively deployed by the most influential chat participants in the MPC corpus. The VCA design, architecture and mode of operation are described in detail in Section 5 of this paper.

2 Related Work

Automated dialogue agents such as the early ELIZA (Weizenbaum, 1966) and PARRY

Proceedings of the 2010 Workshop on Companionable Dialogue Systems, ACL 2010, pages 43–48,
Uppsala, Sweden, 15 July 2010.

(Colby, 1974) could conduct a one-on-one "conversation" with a human using rules and pattern-matching algorithms. More recently, the addition of heuristic pattern matching in A.L.I.C.E (Wallace, 2008) led to development of chat bots using AIML[1] and its variations, such as Project CyN[2]. Most of the work on conversational agents was limited to one-on-one situations, where a single agent converses with a human user, whether to perform a transaction (such as booking a flight or banking transactions) (Hardy et al., 2006) or for companionship (e.g., browsing of family photographs) (Wilks, 2010). Many of these systems were inspired by the challenge of the Turing Test or its more limited variants such as Loebner Prize.

Research in the field of developing a multi-user chat-room agent has been limited. This is somewhat surprising because a multi-user setting makes the agent's task of maintaining conversation far less onerous than in one-on-one situations. In a chat-room, with many users engaged in conversations, it is much easier for an agent to pass as just another user. Indeed, a skillfully designed agent may be able to influence an ongoing conversation.

3 MPC Chat Corpus

The MPC chat corpus is a collection of 20 hours of chat sessions with multiple participants (on average 4), conversing for about 90 minutes in a secure online chat room. The topics of conversation vary from free-flowing chat in the initial collection phase to allow participants to build comfortable a rapport with each other, to specific task-oriented dialogues in the latter phase; such as choosing the right candidate for a job interview from a list of given resumes. This corpus is suitable for our research purposes since the chat sessions were designed around enabling the social phenomena we were interested in modeling.

4 Annotation Scheme

We wished to annotate the data we collected to derive models from language use for social phenomena. These represent complex pragmatic concepts that are difficult to annotate directly, let alone detect automatically. Our approach was to build a multi-level annotation scheme.

In this paper we briefly outline our annotation scheme that consists of three layers: communicative links, dialogue acts, and topic/focus changes. A more detailed description of the annotation scheme will be presented in a future publication.

4.1 Communicative Links

Annotators are asked to mark each utterance in one of three categories – utterance is addressed to a participant or a set of participants, it is in response to a specific prior utterance by another participant or it is a continuation of the participant's own prior utterance. By an utterance, we mean the set of words in a single turn by a participant. In multi-party chat, participants do not generally add addressing information in their utterances and it is often ambiguous to whom they are speaking. Communicative link annotation allows us to accurately map who is speaking to whom in the conversation, which is required for tracking social phenomena across participants.

4.2 Dialogue Acts

At this annotation level, we developed a hierarchy of 20 dialogue acts, based loosely on DAMSL (Allen & Core, 1997) and SWBD-DAMSL (Jurafsky et al., 1997), but greatly reduced and more tuned to dialogue pragmatics. For example, the utterance "It is cold here today" may function as a Response-Answer when given in response to a question about the weather, and would act as an Assertion-Opinion if it is evaluated alone. The dialogue acts, thus augmented, become an important feature in modeling participant behavior for our research purpose. A detailed description of the tags is beyond the scope of this paper.

4.3 Topic and Focus boundaries

The flow of discussion in chat shifts quite rapidly from one topic to another. Furthermore, within each topic (e.g., *music bands*) the focus of conversation (e.g., *dc for cutie*) moves just as rapidly. We distinguish between topic and focus to accommodate both broader thematic shifts and more narrow aspect changes of the topic being discussed. For example, participants might discuss the topic of healthcare reform, by focusing on *President Obama*, and then switch the focus to some particulars of the reform, such as the *"public option"*. Similarly, topics may shift while the focus remains the same (e.g., moving on to Obama's economic policies), although such changes are less common. Annotators typically marked the first mention of a substantive noun phrase as a topic or focus introduction.

[1] http://www.alicebot.org/aiml.html
[2] http://www.daxtron.com/123start.htm?Cyn

The effect of topic change is apparent when a subsequent utterance by another participant is about the same topic. This is a successful attempt at changing the topic. Shown in Figure 1 is an example of topic shift annotated in our data collection.

AA 1: did anyone watch the morning talk shows today (MTP, for example)?
KA 2: nope!
AA 3: I missed them – I was hoping someone else had.
AA 4: My kids tell me the band you're going to hear (dc for cutie) is great.
(TOPIC: music bands, FOCUS: dc for cutie)
KA 5: oh cool! Their lyrics are nice, I think.
(TOPIC: music bands, FOCUS: dc for cutie)
KA 6. what kind of music do you guys listen to?
(TOPIC: music, FOCUS: none)
KN 7: I don't really have a favorite genre….you on youtube right now?
(TOPIC: music, FOCUS: youtube)

Figure 1. A topic change in dialogue, with three participants (AA, KA and KN)

We found this model of topic change fairly consistently exhibited, where the participants would ask an open question, in order to get other participants to respond to them, thereby changing the course of conversation. We collected all utterances marked topic shifts and focus shifts and created a set of templates from them. These templates served as a model for the VCA to utilize when creating a response.

Another model of behavior that we found as a consequence of topic change is topic sustain. This is an instance where the utterance is marked to be on the same topic as the one currently being discussed, for example, utterance 5 in Figure 1. These may be in the form of offering support or agreement with a previous utterance or asking a question about a new in-topic aspect.

We gave our annotators a fair amount of leverage on how to label the topics and how to recognize the focus. Our primary interest was in an accurate detection of topic/focus boundaries and shifts. Of the 14 sessions we selected from the MPC corpus, we selected 10 for annotation, with at least 3 annotators for each session. In Table 1 some of the overall statistics computed from this set are shown. We computed inter-annotator agreement on all three levels of our annotation, i.e. Communication Links, Dialogue Acts and Topic/Focus Shifts. Topic and Focus shifts had the highest inter-annotator agreement scores on different measures such as Krippendorf's Alpha (Krippendorff, 1980) and Fliess' Kappa (Fliess, 1971). In Figure 2, we show inter-annotator agreement measures on Topic/Focus shift annotation for four of the annotated sessions. Krippendorff's Alpha and Fleiss' Kappa measures show inter-annotator agreement on topic shift alone, and Conflated Krippendorff's Alpha measures show the agreement when topic and focus are conflated as one category. With such high degree of agreement, we can reliably derive models of topic shift behavior from our annotated data.

Total Number of Sessions Annotated	10
Number of annotators per file	3
Total Utterances Annotated	4640
Average number of utterances per session	~520
Total topics identified per session	174
Total topic shifts identified per session	344

Table 1. Selected statistics from annotated data set

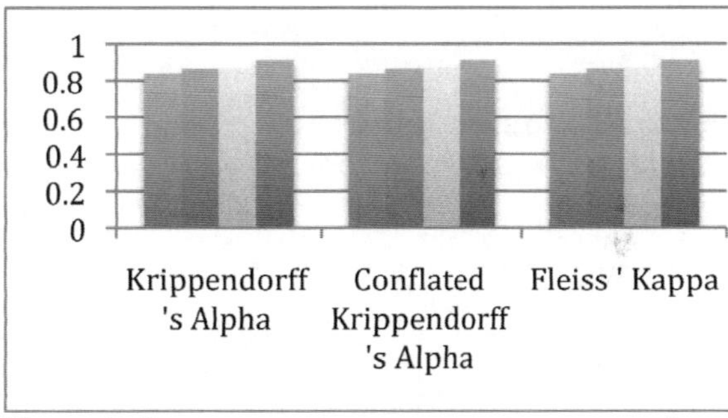

Figure 2. Inter-annotator agreement measures for Topic/Focus shifts

5 VCA Design

A virtual chat agent is an automated program with the ability to respond to utterances in chat. Our VCA is distinctive in its ability to participate in multi-party chat and manage to steer the flow of conversation to a new topic. We exploit the dialogue mechanism underlying HITIQA (Small et al. 2009) to drive the dialogue in VCA.

The topic as defined by the information contained in the participant's utterance is used to mine outside data sources (e.g., a corpus, the web) in order to locate and learn additional information about that topic. The objective is to identify some of the salient concepts that appear associated with the topic, but are not directly mentioned in the utterance. Such associations may be postulated because additional concepts are repeatedly found near the concepts mentioned in the utterance.

An illustrative example found in our annotated corpus is the utterance, "*Lars Ulrich might have a thing or two to say about technology.*" Here, the topic of conversation prior to this utterance was "*technology*" and it was changed to "*music*" after this utterance. Here, "*Lars Ulrich*" is the bridge that connects the two concepts "*technology*" and "*music*" together.

5.1 VCA Architecture

The VCA is composed of the following modules that interact as shown in Figure 3.

5.1.1 Chat Analyzer

Every utterance in chat is first analyzed by the Chat Analyzer component. This process removes stop words, emoticons and punctuation, as well as any participant nicknames from the utterance. We postulate that the remaining content bearing words in the utterance represent the topic of that utterance. We call this analyzed utterance our chat "query" which is sent in parallel to the Document Retrieval and NL Processing component.

5.1.2 Document Retrieval

The document retrieval process retrieves documents from either the web or a test document collection, creating a stable document set for experimental purposes. Currently, the document corpus contains about 1Gb of text data.

5.1.3 Clustering

We cluster the paragraphs in documents retrieved using clustering method in Hardy et al. (Hardy et al., 2009) This process groups the paragraphs containing salient entities into sets of closely associated concepts. From each cluster, we choose the most representative paragraph, usually called the "seed" paragraph for further NL processing. Each seed paragraph and the chat query undergo the same further NL processing sequence.

5.1.4 Natural Language Processing

We process each chat query by performing stemming, part-of-speech tagging and named-entity recognition on it. Each seed paragraph is also run through same three natural language processing tasks. We are using Stanford POS tagger for our part-of-speech tagging. For named entity recognition, we have the ability to choose between BBN's IdentiFinder and AeroText™ (Taylor, 2004).

5.1.5 Framing

We build frames from the entities and attributes found in both the chat query and the paragraphs.. This work extends the concept of framing developed for HITIQA (Small et al, 2009) and COLLANE (Strzalkowski, 2009). Framing provides an informative handle on text, which can be ex-

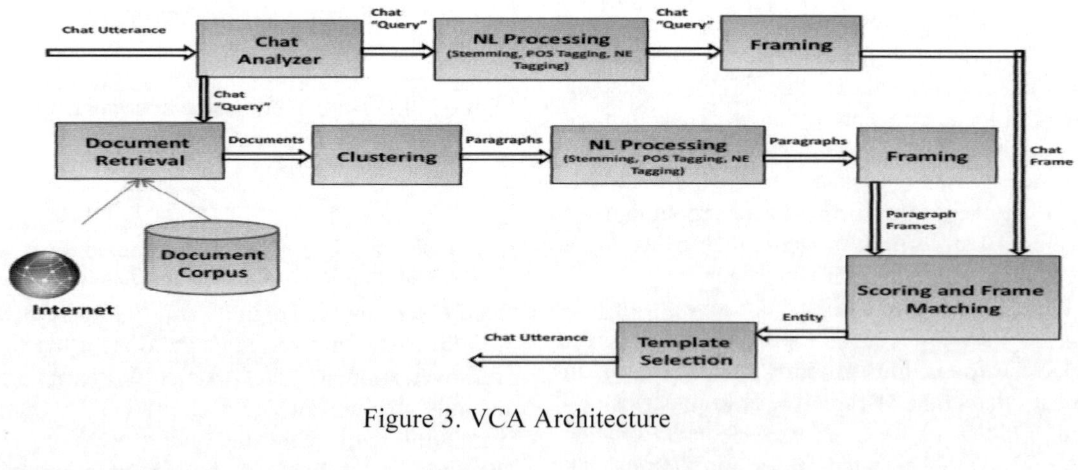

Figure 3. VCA Architecture

ploited to compare the underlying textual representations, as we explain in the next section.

corpus. We use Google AJAX api for our web retrieval process and InQuery (Callan et al., 1992) retrieval engine for our offline mode of operation to retrieve documents from the test corpus. The test document corpus was collected by mining the web for all utterances in our data

5.1.6 Scoring and Frame Matching

Using the information in the frames built in the previous step; we compare the chat query frame built from the chat query, to the frames created from the paragraphs, called paragraph frames. We assign a score for each paragraph frame based on how many attributes and their corresponding values match; in the current version of VCA a very basic approach to counting how many attribute-value pairs match is taken. Of all the paragraph frames we select the highest scoring frames and select the attribute-value pairs that are not part of the chat query frame. For example, as shown in Figure 4a below, the chat utterance "Aruba might be nice!" created the following chat query frame.

[POS]
NNP, Aruba
JJ, nice
[ENT] PLACE

a. Example chat query frame

Aruba Entity List:
VALUE = NASCAR and TYPE = ORGANIZATION and SCORE = 0
VALUE = **Dallas** and TYPE = PLACE and SCORE = 1
VALUE = Mateo and TYPE = PERSON and SCORE = 0

VCA: How about Dallas?

b. Frame Matching, Scoring and Template Selection

Figure 4. From frames to VCA responses

Correspondingly, we select all PLACE type entities from the highest-ranking paragraph frames. These are shown in Figure 4b as Aruba Entity list. The entities "*NASCAR*", "*Women Seeking Men*" and "*Mateo*" are not of entity type – PLACE, we assign them a score of 0. The score is the frequency of occurrence of that entity in the paragraph; in this example it is found to be 1. Assigning scores by frequency of occurrence ensures that the most commonly occurring concept around the one that is being discussed in the chat query utterance will be used to respond with.

5.1.7 Template Selection

Once we have chosen the entity to respond with, we select a template from the set of templates for that entity. These are templates that are created based on the models created from topic change utterances annotated in our data set. For a select group of entities, which are quite frequently encountered in our data collection such as PLACE, PERSON, ORGANIZATION etc., we have a set of templates specific to that entity type. We also have several generic templates that may be used if the entity type does not match the ones that we have selected. For example, a PLACE specific template is "*Have you ever been to _?*" and a PERSON specific template is "*You heard about _?*". Not all templates are formulated as questions. Another example of a generic template is "*_rules!*".

6 Example of VCA Interaction

Figure 5 represents an example of the VCA in action in a simulated environment; the VCA is the participant "renee". We can see how the conversation changes from "*gun laws*" to "*hunting*" after renee's utterance at 11:48 AM.

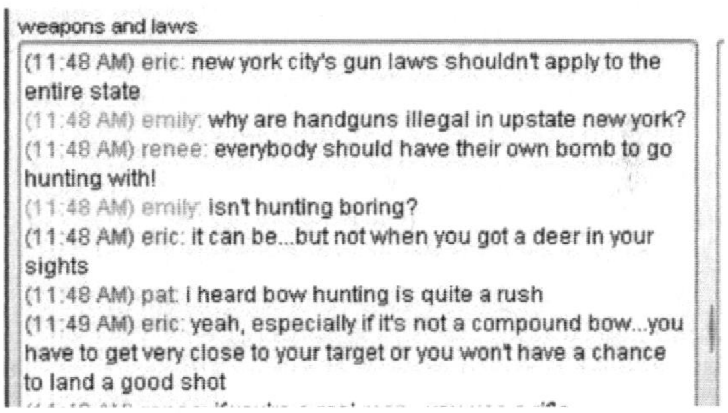

Figure 5. Topic change example

7 Evaluation

We ran two tests of this initial VCA prototype in a public chat-room. VCA was inserted into a public chat-room with multiple participants on two separate occasions. The general topic of discussion during both instances was "*anime*". We have developed an evaluation protocol in order to test the effectiveness of the VCA prototype in a realistic setting. The initial metric of VCA effectiveness is the rate of involvement measured in the number of utterances generated by the VCA during the test period. These utterances are subsequently judged for appropriateness using the metric developed for the Companions Project (Webb, 2010). The actual appropriateness annotation scheme can be quite involved, but for this simple test we reduced the coding to only binary assessment, so that the VCA utterances were annotated as either appropriate or inappropriate, given the content of the utterance and the flow of dialogue thus far. Using this coarse grain evaluation on a live chat segment we noted that the VCA made 9 appropriate utterances and 7 inappropriate utterances, which gives the appropriateness score of 56%. While some of VCA utterances seem inappropriate (i.e., not related to the conversation topic), we noted also that other posters generally tolerated these inappropriate utterances that occurred early in the dialogue. Moreover, these early inappropriate utterances did generate appropriate responses from the human users. This "positive" dynamic changed gradually as the dialogue progressed, when the participants began to ignore VCA's utterances.

While this coarse grained evaluation is useful, our plan is to conduct evaluation experiments by recruiting subjects for chat sessions and inserting the VCA in the discussion. We will measure the impact of the VCA in the chat session by having participants fill out post-session questionnaires, which can elicit their responses regarding (a) if they detect presence of a VCA at any time during the dialogue; (b) who was the VCA; (c) who changed the topic of conversation most often; and so on. Another metric of interest is the level of engagement of the VCA, which can be measured by the number of direct responses to an utterance by the VCA. We are developing the evaluation process, and report on the results in a separate publication.

References

Allen, J. M. Core. (1997). Draft of DAMSL: Dialog Act Markup in Several Layers. http://www.cs.rochester.edu/research/cisd/resources/damsl/

Callan, J. P., W. B. Croft, and S. M. Harding. 1992. *The INQUERY Retrieval System*, in Proceedings of the 3rd Inter- national Conference on Database and Expert Systems.

Colby, K.M, Hilf, F.D, and S. Weber. 1972. Turing-like indistinguishability tests for the validation of a computer simulation of paranoid processes. In: *Artificial Intelligence* , Vol. 3, p. 199-221.

Fleiss, Joseph L. 1971. Measuring nominal scale agreement among many raters. Psychological Bulletin, 74(5):378{382.

Hardy, Hilda, Nobuyuki Shimizu, Tomek Strzalkowski, Ting Liu, Bowden Wise and Xinyang Zhang. 2002. Cross-document summarization by concept classification. In *Proceedings of ACM SIGIR '02 Conference,* pages 121-128, Tampere, Finland.

Hardy, H., A Biermann, R. Bryce Inouye, A. McKenzie, T. Strzalkowski, C. Ursu, N. Webb and M. Wu. 2006. The AMITIES System: Data-Driven Techniques for Automated Dialogue. In Speech Communication 48 (3-4), pages 354-373. Elsevier.

Jurafsky, Dan, Elizabeth Shriberg, and Debra Biasca. (1997). Switchboard SWBD-DAMSL Shallow-Discourse-Function Annotation Coders Manual. http://stripe.colorado.edu/~jurafsky/manual.august1.html

Krippendorff, Klaus. 1980. Content Analysis, an Introduction to its Methodology. Sage Publications, Thousand Oaks, CA.

Samira S., Tomek Strzalkowski, Sarah Taylor and Jonathan Smith (2009) Comparing an Integrated QA system performance - A Preliminary Model. Proceedings of PACLING Conference, Sapporo, Japan.

Shaikh, S., Strzalkowski, T., Broadwell, A., Stromer-Galley, J., Taylor, Sarah and Webb, N. 2010. Proceedings of LREC Conference, Malta.

Sharon Small and Tomek Strzalkowski. 2009. HITIQA: High-Quality Intelligence through Interactive Question Answering. *Journal of Natural Language Engineering*, Vol. 15 (1), pp. 31—54. Cambridge.

Tomek Strzalkowski, Sarah Taylor, Samira Shaikh, Ben-Ami Lipetz, Hilda Hardy, Nick Webb, Tony Cresswell, Min Wu, Yu Zhan, Ting Liu, and Song Chen. 2009. COLLANE: An experiment in computer-mediated tacit collaboration. In Aspects of Natural Language Processing (M. Marciniak and A. Mykowiecka, editors). Springer.

Taylor, Sarah M. 2004. "Information Extraction Tools: Deciphering Human Language." IT Professional. Vol. 06, no. 6, pages: 28-34. November/December, 2004. Online. http://ieeexplore.ieee.org/iel5/6294/30282/01390870.pdf?tp=&arnumber=1390870&isnumber=30282

Wallace, R. 2008. The Anatomy of A.L.I.C.E. In Parsing the Turing Test. (Robert Epstein, Gary Roberts and Grace Beber, editors). Springer.

Webb, N., D. Benyon, P. Hansen and O. Mival. 2010. Evaluating Human-Machine Conversation for Appropriateness. In *Proceedings of the 7th International Conference on Language Resources and Evaluation (LREC2010)*, Valletta, Malta.

Weizenbaum, Joseph. January 1966. "ELIZA — A Computer Program For the Study of Natural Language Communication Between Man And Machine", Communications of the ACM 9 (1): 36–45.

Wilks, Y. 2010. Artificial Companions. In: Y.Wilks (ed.) Close Engagement with Companions: scientific, economic, psychological and philosophical perspectives. John Benjamins: Amsterdam.

Author Index

Association for Computational Linguistics
209 N. Eighth Street
Stroudsburg, Pennsylvania 18360

CURRAN ASSOCIATES INC
proceedings.com